Bob Griese (signature)

GRIESE SPOON

COOKBOOK

by Bob & Shay Griese

A COLLECTION OF FAVORITE
RECIPES SHARED BY
CELEBRITIES AND FRIENDS

Shay (signature)

by Bob & Shay Griese

Front cover photo by Dan Forer of Miami. Pictured is the dining room of Bob and Shay Griese's North Carolina home. This magnificent shot highlights the Blue Ridge Mountain view from their dining room table. Also, featured on the front cover are some of the celebrities that contributed recipes to *The Griese Spoon*.

Back cover photo featuring Bob, Shay and their dog Maggie by Dan Forer of Miami. Also, featured (bottom left) Bob and Shay in the kitchen of their Florida home.

First Printing   2012
Second Printing   2012

Copyright © 2012

For additional copies of
GRIESE SPOON
call 800.548.2537
or go to www.wimmerco.com

WIMMER
cookbooks
A CONSOLIDATED GRAPHICS COMPANY
wimmerco.com   800.548.2537

FOREWORD BY KEITH JACKSON

I am not a connoisseur of anything but I do fancy that I have tasted my fair share of incredible food flavors of all manner of kitchens all over the world.

Couldn't manage some of the language but no matter...shouldn't talk with your mouth full anyway. More than once on a long flight I have put aside the latest best seller to wander with mouth watering pleasure through a cookbook from an innovative mind. And often times those incredible presentations come from the home and the hearth and become legacy in a family. With each generation tinkering with the ingredients it helps more than hinders.

This Book is a collection of tested adventures in culinary prowling by Shay Griese... yep That Griese...and you will find something special on most every page.

So enjoy all the way to the first hiccup!

BOB GRIESE BIOGRAPHY

Bob Griese combined excellence in two distinct areas — on the football field and in the broadcast booth. He was a Hall of Fame quarterback for the Miami Dolphins and then became one of network television's most respected football analysts.

As a collegian, Griese was a two-time All American at Purdue and was voted the All-Time Quarterback for Purdue's first 100 years. He was named to the inaugural class of the Boilermaker Athletic Hall of Fame and is a member of College Football's Hall of Fame.

After his outstanding collegiate career, Griese was drafted fourth overall as the Miami Dolphins' number one pick in 1967. Known as the "thinking man's quarterback" during his brilliant 14-year NFL career with the Dolphins (1967-1980), he was renowned for his poised leadership and ingenious play-calling during their dominance of the NFL in the early 1970s.

Griese led the Dolphins to three straight Super Bowl appearances and back-to-back championships in 1972 and 1973. His greatest accomplishment came in 1972, when he returned from a mid-season injury to lead his team to their "Perfect Season" (17-0) championship season, the only time in NFL history a team went undefeated all year.

Griese, who became the 14th passer to join the NFL's exclusive 25,000-yard club, had a .700 winning percentage (91-39-1) under Miami head coach Don Shula. He appeared in eight NFL All-Star Games, including six Pro Bowls, and was a consensus All-Pro in 1971 and 1977. He was inducted into the Pro Football Hall of Fame in 1990 and his #12 jersey was the first of only three numbers to have been retired by the Dolphins. In 1990 he was one of the original group of players named to the Dolphin Honor Roll and also that year was elected by the fans as the quarterback on the Dolphins' Silver Anniversary all-time team.

"He's probably the most unselfish guy I've ever been around," said Shula. "He got as much of a thrill calling the right running play for a touchdown as he did connecting on a bomb. That's just his makeup." Dolphin founder Joe Robbie felt the same way, calling Griese "the cornerstone of the franchise."

Following his retirement as a player, Griese took his football acumen to the broadcast booth, where he excelled as one of the most insightful football commentators in the industry. He spent 29 years on national television — five with NBC Sports' NFL coverage, and 24 seasons with ABC/ESPN covering college football.

Direct, frank commentary and skillful use of a telestrator during replays helped distinguish Griese as an insightful and enlightening analyst. He worked with the legendary Keith Jackson for twelve years on ABC's weekly coverage of college football, broadcasting the sports' marquee matchups nationally as well as the Fiesta, Sugar, Orange and Rose Bowls and several National Championship Games. During much of that time he also covered the Miami Dolphins' preseason games on television, and starting in 2011 transitioned from his college TV responsibilities to join the Dolphins' regular season radio broadcast team.

Griese serves as Chairman of the Board of Advisors of the Moffitt Cancer Center, is a Board member of the Don Shula Foundation and a senior member of the Orange Bowl Committee. He is a devoted supporter of Judi's House, and he has endowed a football scholarship at his alma mater, Purdue University.

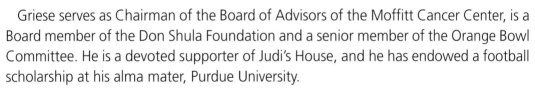

He is the father of three sons, one of whom, Brian, is a retired NFL quarterback. The two co-authored a book, along with Jim Denney, titled "Undefeated" — a biographical account of triumph over great odds, both on the field and off, as their wife/mother succumbed to cancer in 1988, when Brian was only 12. Bob Griese remarried in 1994. He and his wife, Shay Whitney Griese, live in Jupiter, Florida.

DEDICATION AND ACKNOWLEDGEMENTS

This is dedicated to all the people who contributed and worked on this cookbook to benefit Moffitt Cancer Center and Judi's House.

We would like to gratefully acknowledge all our friends and family who generously shared their recipes with us to make this cookbook a lasting contribution to our charities.

A special thanks to Ms. Jean McNamee for editing the recipes for *Griese Spoon*. Thanks again for the many hours of reading and re-reading.

We also extend our warmest appreciation to the team at Wimmer Cookbooks for taking our vision and making it a reality. Special thanks to Maureen Fortune and Jennifer Allison for translating our ideas and putting the pieces together. Thanks to Doug McNeill and Chris Toomey for having the same goals as ours. Both men believed in this project before the outline was ever on paper. Thanks to each and every employee of Mercury/Wimmer that worked on producing Griese Spoon. We appreciate your efforts and will always be grateful.

Proceeds from the sale of *Griese Spoon Cookbook* will benefit the H. Lee Moffitt Cancer Center in Florida and Judi's House in Denver, Colorado.

MOFFITT **Moffitt Cancer Center** opened its doors in 1986. Since then, physicians, scientists, researchers and staff have collaborated to transform the lives of thousands of people who have been impacted by cancer.

Your continued support of our patient care and research efforts has helped Moffitt to reach immeasurable heights. A world-class research and clinical facility, Moffitt Cancer Center uses state-of-the-art equipment throughout its laboratories and clinics to provide the highest possible quality care. Moffitt is the only Florida-based National Cancer Institute and Comprehensive Cancer Center, and its focus on translational research has made an international imprint.

Moffitt has been nationally recognized for developing personalized medicine; this patient-focused approach identifies the needs of patients and their families, allowing clinicians to make decisions based on the clinical and biological characteristics of each individual cancer. The approach seeks to improve patient outcomes as well as access affordable and quality care.

judi's house **Judi's House** was founded by Brian Griese in honor and in memory of his mother who died when he was twelve years old.

The vision of Judi's House is a community in which no child has to feel alone in grief. Our mission is to help children and families who are grieving the death of a loved one find hope and healing within themselves. At Judi's House, an environment of acceptance and understanding allows children and adults in peer support groups to share the experience of loss with others. Judi's House increases awareness and knowledge of grieving children's needs by extending grief support services to schools, faith-based groups, hospices, and other caregivers in the community.

Judi's House is located in Denver, Colorado, and more than 2,600 children and their adult caregivers from the metro area have participated in our groups since we opened our doors in 2002.

SHAY GRIESE BIO

Shay grew up in Canada; her maiden name is Whitney which means horses and universities. She loved the animals, summer jobs at her dad's law offices and back then no concern for food. As she grew older she spent lots of time ski racing and riding, which led to a love for different and healthy fast foods from different countries and friends.

Shay met Bob on an airplane the day he was named to the Hall of Fame and she asked him about food. Since then she makes it a fun way to break the ice with strangers on the plane by asking 2 things they do other than work. Of course, one is sports and the other is do you watch the cooking channels. Without exception, everyone has more interest in food than even sports.

After Shay and Bob were married in 1994 she decided with their friendships and their love for the Moffitt Cancer Center and Judi's House to dedicate the last 2 years to compiling recipes for *Griese Spoon Cookbook*. They should prove to be super!

This book is intended to be a taste and test using your own imagination and your own taste buds.

~Shay

ENJOY IT
LIKE A CELEBRITY

Bob Griese being sacked by
Oakland Raiders Lineman Ben Davidson

Bob Griese

Bob and I met on an American Airlines flight. He was traveling to Vegas and I was stopping in Dallas for my job. Typically humble, Bob didn't tell me why he was headed there and off he went to his connecting flight. I went to a Maverick's game. The next morning, I opened the paper and realized that the night before he was named to the NFL Hall of Fame. It was Super Bowl weekend. Bob had lost his wife to breast cancer 2 years before. Certainly it was sad to see such a nice thing happen without the privilege of sharing it with his wife and the mother of his 3 great boys. After returning, I missed a flight and was delayed in the Miami airport and found out that he was expected in from the greeting press. I went to the gate and met Bob and all his crazy and completely fun friends and a barrage of media to say hello. They squirreled him off to his home in the Coral Gables and I went on to Houston for work on the next flight. I found out later that they had hung banners over his house and T.Peed his trees. They then made him cook these Cuban sandwiches adorned with a cowboy hat. Bob and I were married 4½ years later and I have thankfully inherited his goofball friends, his wonderful boys and their wives and now 7 grandchildren. Enjoy this recipe as have the ESPN, ABC, Channel 10 (Florida) and the Miami Dolphins broadcast crew have.

BOB GRIESE'S CUBAN SANDWICH

1   sweet onion, finely chopped
Green relish
1   loaf Cuban bread
Yellow mustard
Mayonnaise
Spiced pork, sliced
Ham, sliced
Swiss cheese, thinly sliced
Butter

In a bowl, mix onion with equal amount of green relish; set aside. Slice lengthwise bread and remove the soft part leaving a trough. Slather the one side with mustard and the other with mayonnaise. Layer spiced pork and any good ham until the sandwich is fairly thick, about ½ inch. Sprinkle the onion and relish mixture the length of the bread then cover with Swiss cheese. All of the amounts are to your liking. Cut the sandwich in half, butter or spray lightly with a vegetable oil and place in a panini press or a shallow frying pan. Cut the sandwich in 2-inch diagonal pieces and serve.

This Cuban travels well wrapped individually in foil and is excellent as a leftover. If you don't have a press as we didn't years ago, take a cookie sheet and place it on top with a brick on top of that to give it weight and press the sandwich flat. Cook over low heat until the cheese is melting and the bread is toasted. If you use a pan, you will need to flip it to toast the other side.

11

THE BEST TURKEY SANDWICH

2   slices raisin bread
Mayonnaise
Thinly sliced turkey
Cranberry sauce
Orange marmalade

Toast bread lightly; spread with mayonnaise. Add sliced turkey and top with cranberry sauce mixed with orange marmalade. Serve.

SIMPLE SALAD

Romaine
Butter lettuce
Radicchio
Endive
Mild white onion
Sea salt
Fresh ground pepper
Olive oil
Red wine vinegar

Chop romaine, butter lettuce, radicchio, endive, mild white onion and ground sea salt, fresh pepper, good olive oil and red wine vinegar (2-1 ratio) and toss.

McCormick and Alessi make these seasonings sold in the spice department in their own grinder.

SISTER SHARON'S FAVORITE

1   box scalloped potatoes

Onion, finely chopped

4   eggs, beaten or cholesterol-free egg
    product

Dry basil

Pepper, to taste

Sandwich ham, chopped
    (Pesto Parmesan or rosemary
    by Boars Head® is best. See page
    149 for ordering information.)

Shredded Cheddar cheese

Tomatoes, thinly sliced

Preheat oven to 350 degrees.

Butter the bottom of a deep 8x8-inch Teflon pan, or spray with cooking spray to prevent sticking.

Prepare scalloped potatoes according to package directions, reducing the liquid requirement of only the water by half and reserve season packet for later.

In a bowl, mix eggs, basil and pepper. Add season packet from scalloped potato box; mix well. Add ham, cooked potatoes, and a large handful of shredded Cheddar cheese.

Pour mixture in prepared pan until the height is about 2 inches. Bake in preheated oven for 30-45 minutes or until center is firm to touch. Let rest for a few minutes, then sprinkle with shredded cheese of your choice; cover with aluminum foil for a few minutes to melt cheese and serve.

My sister reminded me of this one that I made for her 30 years ago. Since she is a great cook, I was honored that she would consider it one of her favorites. Hopefully, it is still reliably good.

BRUSHETTA

1 loaf baguette
Olive oil
Tomato, finely chopped
Onion
Goat or blue cheese

Slice baguette loaf in ¼-inch increments. Brush the top with olive oil and place on a cookie sheet covered with foil. Spoon on tomatoes, onion and goat or blue cheese mixture and bake at 300 degrees for about 5-10 minutes.

Brushetta is difficult to eat if the bread is too toasty. Try to get it very lightly toasted.
~Shay Griese

SHRIMP IN BEER WITH RED ONIONS APPETIZER

3   bottles regular beer

Seafood seasoning, I use Old Bay®

Fresh or frozen shrimp, cooked and
    peeled

Mayonnaise

Juice of ½ lemon

Red onion, finely chopped

Green onions, finely chopped

In a medium stockpot, add beer and add lots of seafood seasoning or Old Bay; bring to a boil. Add cooked and peeled shrimp and bring back to boil for about 5-10 minutes. Drain and let cool; remove the tails. Pour into a mixing bowl and add seafood seasoning or a Chef Prudhomme preference, mayonnaise to lightly cover, and lemon juice into the mixture. Add red onion and mix. Refrigerate. Cut the end off the other half of lemon and place in the center of a platter. Using large lettuce leaves, make a bed for the shrimp. Take toothpicks and stick them in the lemon. Arrange chilled shrimp then sprinkle with green onions.

MINI PIZZA APPETIZERS

1   package Pepperidge Farms®
    crescent rolls

1   (8-ounce) package cream cheese

1   package sliced pepperoni

Place crescent rolls on a cooking sheet and pinch crescent rolls together to make a flat square. Spread with cream cheese and arrange pepperoni liberally and roll up into a log. Bake at 300 degrees until golden brown. Remove and slice into easy to handle pieces.

Bridgeford® pepperoni is best but you can use a seasoned ham, too.

~Shay Griese

Brian Griese

DENVER BRONCOS

Former American football quarterback and current radio color commentator for the Denver Broncos. He has also played for the Miami Dolphins, Chicago Bears and Tampa Bay Buccaneers. A Pro Bowl selection with the Broncos in 2000, Griese earned a Super Bowl ring with the team, as the third-string quarterback in Super Bowl XXXIII.

DID YOU KNOW?

Brian Griese is the son of NFL quarterback Bob Griese. He was born in Miami, Florida and attended Christopher Columbus High School in Miami, playing football, basketball, and golf. In football, he won All-State third team honors as a senior.

Griese played college football at the University of Michigan from 1993 to 1997. The Denver Broncos selected Griese in the third round of the 1998 NFL Draft. He became a Super Bowl champion in 1998.

In June 2003, he signed with the Miami Dolphins. In 2004, Griese signed with and performed well for the Tampa Bay Buccaneers, and provided a catalyst for the jumpstart of the Tampa offense. On March 21, 2006, he signed a five year contract with the Chicago Bears. The Bears went on to win the 2006 NFC Championship. On March 3, 2008, Griese was traded to the Tampa Bay Buccaneers. In 2009, Brian Griese decided to retire from football.

Since 2009, Griese has been employed by ESPN, working as an analyst on the network's college football coverage. Griese also serves as radio color commentator for KOA (AM)'s coverage of Denver Broncos Football.

Griese founded Judi's House in 2002 in memory of his mother who died when he was 12 years old. The center helps grieving children and families by offering grief counseling and peer support groups to share the experience of loss with others. Judi's House increases awareness and knowledge of grieving children's needs by extending grief support services to schools, community-based organizations, faith-based groups, hospices, and other caregivers in the community. As of October 2011, Judi's House has served more than 4,000 children and their adult caregivers from the Denver area since opening.

Brian's handwritten menu.

judi's house
HOPE AND HEALING FOR GRIEVING CHILDREN

BRIAN GRIESE

Kids Menu at: "The Griese Spoon"

Cheese Burgers & Strawberry Shakes
(As Served at Judi's House Backyard Community BBQ's)

Cheeseburgers (makes 6)

- 1.5 lb Ground Beef
- 1/4 cup Worcestershire
- 1 Egg
- 1/2 cup Bread Crumbs
- 2 Tablespoon Garlic Powder
- Salt & Pepper
- 6 slices Cheddar Cheese
- 6 Hamburger Buns

1. Mix All ingredients in a large Bowl and then form 6 patties.
2. Grill Burgers over Medium-High Heat for 3 minutes, then Turn and Cook 4-6 min longer. Add Cheese + Cover 1 min then Remove.

Brian's Twist

Season patties with Tony's Creole Seasoning before Grilling and Top with Lettuce, Sweet Onion, Dill Pickle + Mustard!

Strawberry Shakes (makes 10 glasses)

1- 28oz. Bag Frozen Strawberries
1/2 Cup Confectioners' Sugar
4 cups Plain Yogurt
1 cup Light Cream or Whole Milk

1. Place Berries, Sugar, and Cream in Blender and Blend.
2. Add Yogurt + Blend until Frothy + Serve!

Drew Brees

Brees is the quarterback for the New Orleans Saints of the National Football League. He has been selected to the Pro Bowl six times in his career and was named the NFL's Comeback Player of the Year in 2004, the Offensive Player of the Year in 2008, and the MVP of Super Bowl XLIV.

WHITE BEAN CHILI

2	tablespoons oil, or olive oil
1	large onion, chopped
1	(4-ounce) can chopped green chiles
2	teaspoons garlic powder
2	teaspoons salt
2	teaspoons ground cumin
2	teaspoons ground oregano
2	teaspoons ground coriander
¼	teaspoon cayenne pepper
3	(15-ounce) cans great Northern white beans, undrained
2	(5.2-ounce) cans chicken, drained
2	(15-ounce) cans chicken broth

In a large pot, heat oil over medium heat; add onion and sauté until brown. Add next 7 ingredients; stir until blended. Stir in remaining ingredients and return to a boil. Reduce heat, and simmer 20 minutes or until heated through.

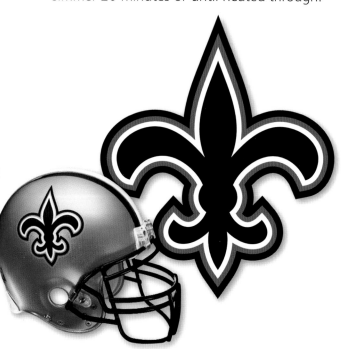

DID YOU KNOW?

Drew Brees was named after Drew Pearson, wide receiver for Dallas Cowboys. He was born in Dallas and attended Westlake High School. He attended Purdue from 1997-2000 and was a member of the Sigma Chi Fraternity.

Brees was selected in the 2001 draft, chosen by the San Diego Chargers as the first pick of the second round. He played in his first professional game on November 4, 2001 against the Kansas City Chiefs. He won the starting job over Doug Flutie during training camp before the start of the 2002 season. Brees started all 16 games for the Chargers during the 2002 season.

Brees has been selected to the Pro Bowl six times in his career – with the Chargers in 2004, Saints in 2006, 2008, 2009, 2010, and 2011. He was named the NFL's Comeback Player of the Year in 2004, and the MVP of Super Bowl XLIV. Some of his other accomplishments include AP Male Athlete of the Year, Sportsman of the Year, and Co-Walter Payton Man of the Year Award in 2006.

In the first game of the 2009 season, he set a career-high and franchise-tying record with six touchdown passes.

In 2011, Drew passed Dan Marino's record on his single season passing leader with 5,476 yards. He had the most completions of 468, most 300 yard passing games (13) and most consecutive 300 yard passing games (7).

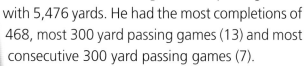

SUPER BOWL XLIV

DREW BREES

CRAB OR SHRIMP MARTINI

Iceberg lettuce, finely chopped or
    prepackage shredded lettuce

Small shrimp or crab

Thousand Island or French dressing

Capers

Lemon or lime, cut in wedges

Place lettuce in a martini glass. In a bowl, mix shrimp or crabmeat with Thousand Island or French dressing. Spoon a serving into glass and garnish with capers and a lemon or lime wedge on the rim.

HERBED PECANS

6 tablespoons butter
4 teaspoons dried rosemary
⅛ teaspoon dried basil
1 tablespoon salt
½ teaspoon cayenne pepper
4 cups pecan halves

In a large saucepan, melt butter. Add seasonings and stir. Remove from heat. Add pecans and toss to coat well. Do not break nuts. Arrange nuts in single layer in jelly-roll pan. Scrape any remaining herb mixture over nuts. Bake in preheated 325 degree oven for 10-12 minutes or until browned. Stir gently 2 or 3 times. Serve warm or at room temperature. Once cooled, they freeze divinely in small plastic bags, just heat 30 seconds in the microwave to bring out the aroma, or simply bring to room temperature and serve.

Mack Brown

Brown is the head coach of The University of Texas at Austin Longhorn football team. He was inducted into the Texas Hall of Fame on February 29, 2012, in Waco, Texas. Prior to his head coach position at Texas, Brown was head coach at Appalachian State, Tulane, and North Carolina. Brown is credited with revitalizing the Texas and North Carolina football programs. In 2006, he was awarded the Paul "Bear" Bryant Award for "Coach of the Year". On November 27, 2008, Brown achieved his 200th career win, making him the first Texas coach to reach that mark.

TEXAS

SHRIMP AND GRITS

4 cups water

Salt and pepper

1 cup stone-ground grits

3 tablespoons butter

2 cups shredded sharp Cheddar cheese

1 pound shrimp, peeled and deveined

6 slices bacon, chopped

4 teaspoons lemon juice

2 tablespoons chopped parsley

1 cup thinly sliced scallions

1 large clove garlic, minced

In a medium saucepan, bring water to a boil. Add salt and pepper. Add grits and cook until water is absorbed, about 20-25 minutes. Remove from heat and stir in butter and cheese.

Rinse shrimp and pat dry. Fry bacon in a large skillet until browned; drain well. In the same skillet with bacon drippings, add shrimp. Cook until shrimp turns pink. Add lemon juice, chopped bacon, parsley, scallions, and garlic. Sauté for 3 minutes.

Spoon grits into serving bowl. Add shrimp mixture and mix well. Serve immediately.

DID YOU KNOW?

Mack began his full-time coaching career in 1975 at Southern Mississippi. In his 39 years of coaching, 28 of those years as a head coach, he enters his 14th season as the head coach of the Texas Longhorns. He has brought enthusiasm back to the UT program while wowing everyone from recruits to supporters. "Mack has helped bring back the pride in Texas Football".

In 13 seasons, Brown's Longhorns squads have featured a Heisman Trophy winner, two runners-up and a third-place Award winner, three WCFF Player of the Year Award winners, two Doak Walker Award winners, two Thorpe Award winners, a Butkus Award winner, a Lombardi Award winner, two Manning Award winners, a Hendricks Award winner, 51 All-Americans, 64 first-team All-Big 12 selections, five Big 12 Offensive Players, and the list goes on.

Texas has lost only 10 road games in Mack Brown's 12-year tenure with two of them coming in his first three games. In the 27 drafts during Brown's time as a head coach, the NFL has picked 102 of his student-athletes.

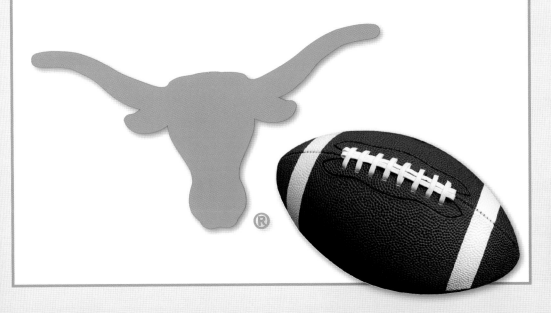

MACK BROWN

Kenny Chesney

Contemporary country star Kenny Chesney didn't have the immediate breakout success that many of his peers enjoyed upon signing with major labels, but gradually built up a significant following via hard work, pop-friendly ballads, and a likable, average-guy personality.

TACKLE BOX FILMS

Bob Griese

This is a note to say thank you for your help and participation in "The Boys of Fall" project. Being involved with this project, and the journey it has taken us on, has been nothing short of amazing. As you will see, this is a very special project and we really appreciate you being a part of it.

A copy of the music video is enclosed for your viewing pleasure. Enjoy and thanks again for being a part of "The Boys of Fall".

Sincerely,

Kenny Chesney

Shaun Silva

DID YOU KNOW?

Chesney was born in Knoxville, TN, in 1968 and raised in the nearby small town of Luttrell, better known as the home of Chet Atkins. He grew up listening to both country and rock & roll, but didn't get serious about music until college, when he studied marketing at East Tennessee State University. He received a guitar as a Christmas present and set about practicing, and was soon performing with the college bluegrass band. He soon started writing songs as well and played for tips in local venues — most often a Mexican restaurant — every night he could; additionally, he managed to sell 1,000 copies of a self-released demo album. After graduation in 1991, he moved to Nashville and became the resident performer at The Turf, a rougher honky tonk in the city's historic district. While he gained experience, it wasn't the sort of place where he'd be discovered, and in 1992, he moved on to a publishing deal with Acuff-Rose. From there he landed a record contract with Capricorn and released his debut album, *In My Wildest Dreams*, in late 1993.

KEY LIME PIE

4   teaspoons grated lime zest

½   cup fresh lime juice (3 to 4 limes)

4   egg yolks

1   (14-ounce) can sweetened
        condensed milk

1¼ cups graham cracker crumbs

½   cup sugar

5   tablespoons unsalted butter, melted

1   (8-ounce) tub whipped topping,
        thawed

Sliced limes, to garnish

Grate lime zest from the whole limes and set aside. Then, slice limes in half and squeeze out the juice, being careful not to include any pits.

In a bowl, whisk egg yolks and lime zest together. Beat in milk and juice; set aside at room temperature until it thickens, approximately 10 minutes.

Preheat oven to 325 degrees.

In a separate bowl, mix graham cracker crumbs and sugar. Add butter and stir with a fork until well blended. Pour crumb mixture into a 9-inch pie pan. Beginning with the sides of the pan, press mixture around the sides and the bottom. Try using the bottom of a measuring cup to make sure the graham cracker mixture forms a firm crust on the bottom of the pan.

Bake on the center rack in preheated oven for about 15 minutes unit crust is lightly brown. Remove and let cool to room temperature.

Pour lime filling into crust, spread evenly, and bake for 15 minutes until the center sets, but still wiggles when shaken.

Remove from oven and cool to room temperature. After the pie has cooled to room temperature, spread whipped topping on top. You can use thinly sliced limes on top to garnish.

Refrigerate for at least 3 hours until well chilled.

PASTA ROBERTO

Spinach

Olive oil

Asparagus tips

Cherry tomatoes

Garlic clove, chopped

Black or green olives

Capers

Linguine

Sea salt and pepper to taste

Parmesan cheese

Sauté spinach in olive oil until slightly wilted. Set aside. In the same pan at medium-low heat, sauté asparagus tips, cherry tomatoes and fresh chopped garlic until asparagus is fork tender. If the garlic burns to a brown color, remove the garlic and discard it. The oil will retain the garlic flavor but burned garlic is bitter. Combine with black or green olives and capers.

Boil fresh linguine until al dente; drain. Place linguine in a large mixing bowl then add olive oil, sea salt, and pepper; toss. Add veggies and toss again. Serve in a shallow bowl and sprinkle with Parmesan cheese.

Bob's favorite appetizer! The capers and olives will go to the bottom of the bowl when tossing; just fish them out with a spoon and put on top of the pasta.
~Shay Griese

PIZZA

1   thin pre-made pizza crust
1   jar pizza sauce
Shredded mozzarella cheese
Spinach, chopped
Ham, thinly sliced
Mushrooms, thinly sliced
Onion, thinly sliced
1   package thin sliced pepperoni
Pineapple, finely chopped

Place pizza crust on pizza pan; cover lightly with sauce all the way to the edge. Sprinkle with mozzarella cheese. Add chopped spinach, ham, mushrooms, onion, and more shredded cheese; top with pepperoni. Bake according to pizza crust directions. Remove from oven and top with pineapple.

Mike Ditka

Ditka is a former American football NFL player, television commentator, and coach. Ditka coached the Chicago Bears for 11 years and New Orleans Saints for three years. Ditka and Tom Flores are the only two people to win Super Bowls as a player, an assistant coach, and a head coach. Ditka was the only individual to participate in both of the last two Chicago Bears' championships, as a player in 1963, and as head coach in 1985.

TAILGATER'S PORK CHOPS WITH GRILLED HONEY–GLAZED CINNAMON APPLES

FOR THE PORK CHOPS

4	cups orange juice
1	cup soy sauce
2	tablespoons chopped garlic
½	cup Dijon mustard
½	cup honey
1	teaspoon cayenne pepper
8	(1-inch) thick pork rib chops

In a mixing bowl, whisk together orange juice, soy sauce, garlic, mustard, honey, and cayenne pepper. Pour over pork chops and marinate in the refrigerator for 12-24 hours. Remove pork from marinade; discard marinade. Season pork with salt and pepper and grill for 8-10 minutes, turning once.

FOR THE APPLES

1	cup butter
1½	tablespoons cinnamon
3	tablespoons honey
4	Granny Smith apples, cored and sliced ¼-inch thick

Dash salt and ground black pepper

In a small saucepan, heat butter, cinnamon, and honey over low heat until melted, stirring constantly. Season apples with salt and pepper; place slices on hot grill. Grill apple slices about 2 minutes on each side while brushing with butter mixture.

DID YOU KNOW?

Michael Keller Ditka played for the Chicago Bears 1961-1966, Philadelphia Eagles 1967-1968, and Dallas Cowboys 1969-1972.

He was the No. 1 draft pick of the Chicago Bears in 1961. He earned All-NFL honors four straight seasons from 1961 through 1964.

In 1967, Ditka was traded to the Philadelphia Eagles. An injury in the second game that year aborted his consecutive-game streak at 86. He missed eight games in two years with the Eagles before moving on to the Dallas Cowboys in 1969. The fiercely determined and competitive Ditka regained much of his old form in four years in Dallas. His best campaign there was in 1971 when the Cowboys won their first Super Bowl championship. Ditka had 30 receptions that year and he scored the final touchdown in Dallas' 24-3 win over the Miami Dolphins in Super Bowl VI.

At the time of his retirement after the 1972 season, he ranked second among all tight ends in receptions.

MIKE DITKA

"You're never a loser until you quit trying."

~Ditka Quote

Sam Donaldson

Donaldson is a reporter and news anchor, serving with ABC News from 1967 to the present, best known as the network's White House Correspondent (1977-89 & 1998-99) and as a panelist and later co-anchor of the network's Sunday Program "This Week." Over the years, Sam has received numerous honors for his contribution to broadcast journalism: the Broadcaster of the Year award from the National Press Foundation; Best White House Correspondent honors in 1985, and consecutive Best Television Correspondent honors in the four following years from the Washington Journalism Review; three George Foster Peabody Awards and four Emmy Awards. Today, Sam Donaldson lives in McLean, Virginia with his wife, television reporter Jan Smith. Retired from day-to-day journalism, he can still be seen on many Sunday mornings as a guest panelist on ABC's This Week.

abc NEWS

THE WHITE HOUSE
WASHINGTON

ENCHILADAS

Cooking oil

1   can Hatch red chile sauce,
       mild or strong

Salt

Corn tortillas

1-1½ cups Longhorn Cheddar cheese,
       shredded

1   yellow onion, finely diced

Fresh cilantro

Sour cream, soft yolk, or cooked egg,
       for garnish

This recipe will curl the hair and tickle the fancy of every man and woman jack alive. If you haven't tasted Donaldson enchiladas, you don't know the meaning of the phrase "The Big Enchilada!"

~Sam Donaldson Quote

Preheat oven to 315 degrees.

In a skillet, heat oil to moderate heat. In a saucepan, on very low heat, pour chile sauce and season lightly with salt.

Using tongs, place a flat tortilla in hot oil until it is soft; do not over cook or it will fall apart. Dip soft tortilla into the sauce and finally place it flat in a glass baking dish. Sprinkle a light covering of cheese on tortilla; add a moderate covering of onions on top. Repeat the process with a second and third tortilla. On the top tortilla after covering with cheese and onion, sprinkle 2-3 sprigs chopped cilantro.

When all the servings are prepared spoon some of the chile sauce onto each stack of tortillas. Bake tortillas in preheated oven for 12 minutes.

Serve immediately with sour cream or soft yolk, cooked egg on top. May also serve with refried beans or chopped green chiles.

I'm from the Southwest where enchiladas are the favorite food (at least mine). If you really want the authentic recipe to be served on a linoleum table cover in an adobe "hole in the wall" café, you will have to make your own corn tortillas. Whip up a batch of chile sauce from scratch, use yellow onions direct from the field, and Longhorn Cheddar cheese freshly packaged. But who has the time or expertise to do that?

So, using store bought ingredients, here is the recipe for two to four servings of flat enchiladas (the rolled kind are for outlanders).

CHILE

2 pounds sirloin lean beef

Onions

Garlic

Mushrooms

1 large can tomato juice

1 can Rotel® Chili Fixin's Seasoned diced tomatoes and green chiles

1 can red beans

Elbow pasta

1 package McCormick's chili powder, optional

In a large skillet, sauté beef, onions, garlic, and mushrooms. Add ½ can of the tomato juice and reserve the other half as needed while cooking. Cook for 1 hour. Add Rotel Chili Fixin's. Add more tomato sauce as needed but try to cook for a couple of hours if possible. Add red beans at the 15 minute warning. If the chili is preferred wet, serve. If not, at the 15 minute warning, add elbow pasta to soak up liquid, and the pasta needs to be soft. You can eyeball this chili according to your taste by adding more liquid. Rotel should not be drained.

Warning: Rotel is spicy...Original Rotel is much milder with a nice effect. Add package of chili powder in case you want more chili flavor bang.

OPEN FACE REUBEN SANDWICH

1   can or jar sauerkraut
Seasoned corn beef, sliced
Turkey slices
Rye bread slices
Thousand Island dressing
Swiss cheese
Mustard, good grainy

In a skillet, heat sauerkraut and boil off the liquid to get the sauerkraut fairly dry. Set aside. Heat slices of either thinly sliced seasoned corn beef or turkey, or both together if you like. Preheat oven to broiler. Using a toaster, toast a couple slices of rye bread and place on a plate. Spread with Thousand Island dressing; add meat. Cover with lots of sauerkraut and finish with slices of Swiss cheese. Put under the broiler until cheese is melted but not burned. Serve with extra dressing and good grainy mustard on the side.

CHICK FILL EH ON A BUN

Olive oil

1   Tyson® breast chicken fillet

1   soft bun

Mustard

Dill pickles

In a saucepan, heat olive oil to medium heat. Add chicken fillet and heat until toasty warm. Serve on a warmed soft bun with mustard and extra dill pickles.

Bob's favorite and easy to make!

~Shay

EASIEST QUICHE

1   bag Stouffer's® spinach soufflé
1   bag cream corn soufflé
½   onion, thinly sliced and chopped
Sandwich ham, cut in bite-size pieces
1   large package Swiss cheese, divided
3-4 eggs, well beaten
Salt and pepper, to taste
1   ready to bake pie shell
Tomatoes, thinly sliced

Preheat oven to 300 degrees. Mix together in a medium bowl, spinach, cream corn soufflé, onion, ham, Swiss cheese, eggs, salt, and pepper. Pour mixture in ready to bake pie shell, or unroll pre-made pie crust in a pie pan. Leave room for expansion while cooking. Lay a piece of aluminum foil over pie. This is to keep the crust from browning too fast. Cook for 45 minutes, then check to see if the middle still looks raw, and if so, keep covered and keep going. When the center is firm to your touch, you will be ready to add thinly sliced tomatoes and a sprinkle of Swiss cheese on top with the cover off. If the crust is brown to your liking, turn off the heat and slightly open the oven door so it can stay warm and rest.

This is a quiche that even real men eat! The pre-made pie crusts freeze very well and don't stick in a glass pie plate which I prefer for this recipe. Also, this is a quiche that with enough eggs can handle lots of variation in meat and vegetable additions.

Roger Goodell

Roger is the Commissioner of the National Football League (NFL), having been chosen to succeed the retiring Paul Tagliabue on August 8, 2006. He was chosen over four finalists for the position, winning a close vote on the fifth ballot before being unanimously approved by acclamation of the owners. He officially began his tenure on September 1, 2006, just prior to the beginning of the 2006 NFL season. As Commissioner, he is also President of NFL Charities. Many commentators have described him as "the most powerful man in sports."

SPICY MAPLE SALMON

6   tablespoons maple syrup
2   tablespoons fresh minced ginger
2   cloves garlic, minced
2   teaspoons hot red pepper flakes, or to taste
½   cup water
¼   teaspoon salt
4   salmon fillets

Combine syrup, ginger, garlic, red pepper flakes, water, and salt in a small saucepan. Simmer until reduced to about ½ cup.

Brush salmon fillets with sauce and broil about 10 minutes, depending on thickness.

From intern to COO

Goodell's career in the NFL began in 1982 as an administrative intern in the league office in New York under then – Commissioner Pete Rozelle – a position secured through an extensive letter-writing campaign to the league office and each of its then 28 teams. In 1983, he joined the New York Jets as an intern, but returned to the league office in 1984 as an assistant in the public relations department.

In 1987, Goodell was appointed assistant to the president of the American Football Conference (Lamar Hunt), and under the tutelage of Commissioner Paul Tagliabue filled a variety of football and business operations roles, culminating with his appointment as the NFL's Executive Vice President and Chief Operating Officer in December, 2001.

As the NFL's COO, Goodell took responsibility for the league's football operations and officiating, as well as supervised league business functions. He headed NFL Ventures, which oversees the league's business units, including media properties, marketing and sales, stadium development and strategic planning.

Mr. Goodell has been instrumental in many league accomplishments including expansion, realignment, stadium development, ad international development, launch of the NFL Network, negotiations for the NFL's television agreements and the Collective Bargaining Agreement with the NFL Players Association.

He serves on the boards of the national and New York chapters of Big Brothers & Big Sisters, and is an officer of NFL Charities, the league's charitable foundation.

ROGER GOODELL

CONEY ISLAND HOT DOG

2   tablespoons butter
1   package all beef hot dogs
1   package hot dog buns
Mustard
Sweet onion, finely chopped
Tomato, finely chopped

In a fry pan, add butter and ½-inch water so the butter does not burn on medium heat. Slice hot dogs with 4 diagonal slices on 2 sides about the length of your fingernail. Place in hot water; cover briefly to let the dogs plump. Then remove the cover. Meantime, wrap the buns in foil and place in the oven to soften and warm about 150-200 degrees. Boil the hot dogs until the water is gone and they will start to brown in the butter remaining. Serve with mustard, chopped onion, and tomato.

This can be made as a kraut dog; just leave off the onion and drain the sauerkraut well, for chili dog leave off everything but the onion. Make sure to use a superior all beef hot dog.

~Shay Griese

Jon Gruden

1985 Hooters "Shucker & Shaker" coach and TV analyst. With very little technical assistance by: Ed Droste co-founder of Hooters Restaurants, Moffitt Cancer Center Foundation Chair.

WORLD FAMOUS HOOTERS WINGS

5   pounds fresh, never frozen chicken wings (skin and flappers on)

1   (12-ounce) jar Hooters Wing Sauce* (medium or hot)

1   package Hooters Secret Breading

1   top ranked QB (always a must)

Pure vegetable oil

Blue cheese dressing (as close to homemade as possible)

1   bundle cold celery sticks

Bread chicken wings in Hooters Secret Breading and refrigerate for 15 minutes.

In a deep fryer, heat oil to 350 degrees, drop in the wings and cook until golden brown; wings may begin to float.

Cut ice cold celery sticks at precisely 4 inches in length and serve with homemade blue cheese dressing in serving cups.

Place cooked wings in a lidded container and add Hooters Wing Sauce at room temperature. Gently shake the wings with a rolling motion until covered thoroughly in delicious sauce.

Gruden Tip: Don't bruise the wings.

Remove wings from the container with tongs and place on a wood-like plate. Serve unused sauce in a cup for dipping.

Ed Droste Tip: Wings go good with beer.

Hooters Wing Sauce can be purchased at www.originalhooters.com/hooters-foods

Jon David Gruden is the former head coach of the Tampa Bay Buccaneers for seven seasons and prior to that, the Oakland Raiders for four seasons. In his first year as the head coach of Tampa Bay, the Buccaneers won Super Bowl XXXVII. At the time, Gruden was the youngest head coach ever to win a Super Bowl. Gruden currently serves as one of two color commentators on ESPN Monday Night Football along with Ron Jaworski.

In 2008, Gruden was rewarded with a contract extension through the 2011 season. On November 30, Gruden earned his 100th win against the New Orleans Saints.

In May 2009, Gruden was hired by ESPN to serve as a color analyst on Monday Night Football telecasts. He has also served as an analyst for ESPN's coverage of postseason college football games, helping to call the 2010 Rose Bowl and 2010 BCS National Championship Game on ESPN Radio and the 2011 Outback Bowl and 2011 Orange Bowl on ESPN television. He has recently signed a contract extension with ESPN, beginning in September 2012, which will lengthen his tenure with the broadcasting company for another five years.

BOB'S BREAKFAST GRANOLA

Butter, unsalted

Slivered almonds, unsalted

Honey

Whole original oats

Raisins

Cranraisins

Dried prunes

Shredded coconut

Blueberries, strawberries, raspberries,
    bananas, your choice

Skim milk

Combine butter, almonds, honey, and oats in a skillet and toast. Add raisins, cranraisins, dried prunes, or anything else you like and finish with shredded coconut. Store in a container in the refrigerator. Add fresh fruit of your choice upon serving with skim milk.

Store bought granola is salty and expensive. Easily you can duplicate it — just keep in mind that keeping it cool preserves the butter.

~Shay Griese

Bryant Gumbel

Bryant is an American television journalist and sportscaster. He is best known for his 15 years as co-host of NBC's The Today Show. From 1975 until January 1982 (when he left The Today Show) Gumbel returned to sportscasting for NBC when he hosted the prime time coverage of the 1988 Summer Olympics from Seoul.

Now he hosts HBO's Real Sports with Bryant Gumbel.

CREOLE STUFFED MIRLITONS

3	mirlitons (a.k.a. chayote squash)
4	tablespoons butter
½	pound ground pork sausage
1	onion, chopped
4	garlic cloves, minced
1	bell pepper, chopped
½	pound shrimp, deveined and chopped
1	teaspoon salt
½	teaspoon black pepper
½	teaspoon red pepper flakes
2	tablespoons chopped parsley
½-¾	cup bread crumbs

Cut mirlitons in half and remove seeds. Place in a pot of water and boil approximately 15 minutes, until tender. Drain and let cool.

Scoop out the pulp. Take care to keep the shells intact. Set shells and pulp aside.

Melt butter in large heavy skillet over medium heat.

Add sausage and onions. Sauté until onions are soft.

Add garlic, bell pepper and mirliton pulp...mix and mash well.

Add shrimp, salt, black pepper, red pepper, and parsley; blend well.

Cook mixture for 15-20 minutes, adding bread crumbs gradually to absorb water and lighten mixture.

Remove from heat, fill shells with mixture, top with bread crumbs, and place in baking dish.

One of Gumbel's more memorable moments during his time at NBC Sports occurred in 1982, when he was on-site for the "Epic in Miami" NFL playoff game between the San Diego Chargers and Miami Dolphins. At the end of the game, Gumbel told the viewing audience "If you didn't like this football game then you don't like football!"

Gumbel's work on *Today* earned him several Emmys and a large group of fans. He is the second longest serving co-host of Today, serving 2 months less than Katie Couric. Gumbel stepped down from the show on January 3, 1997 after 15 years.

Gumbel has concentrated most of his energy recently on his duties as host of HBO's acclaimed investigative series Real Sports with Bryant Gumbel (a show that he has hosted since 1995). HBO's web page claims that *Real Sports* has been described as "flat out TV's best sports program" by the Los Angeles Times. Also according to *HBO, Real Sports* has earned 15 sports Emmys, and a 2006 Alfred I. duPont-Columbia University Award for broadcast journalism, the first time in the award's history that it was given to a sports program.

BRYANT GUMBEL

Bobby Hull

Bobby is regarded as one of the greatest ice hockey players of all time and perhaps the greatest left winger to ever play the game. In his 23 years in the National Hockey League and World Hockey Association, he played for the Chicago Black Hawks, Winnipeg Jets and Hartford Whalers.

CORNY DIP

1	small can chopped green chiles, drained
1	small can chopped jalapeño peppers, drained
1	can white and yellow whole kernel corn, drained
1	can corn with red and green peppers, drained
2	cups shredded Cheddar cheese
4	ounces shredded pepper Jack cheese
¼	cup chopped green onion
¾	cup sour cream
¾	cup mayonnaise
⅛	teaspoon sugar

Mix all ingredients together and serve.

CHICKEN DIP

8   ounces cream cheese, softened

1   (13-ounce) can chicken breast,
        drained and crumbled

¼-½ teaspoon Franks Hot Sauce

    Blue cheese or ranch dressing

2   cups shredded mozzarella cheese

Spread cream cheese on bottom of an 8x8-inch glass baking dish. Add crumbled chicken breast pieces. Drizzle chicken with hot sauce. Spread blue cheese or ranch dressing on top of hot sauce. Prick with fork so dressing can flow to bottom. Top with mozzarella cheese. Bake at 375 degrees for 25-30 minutes, until brown and bubbly.

Hull was famous for his blonde hair, blinding skating speed, and having the hardest shot, earning him the nickname "the Golden Jet." He possessed the most feared slapshot of his day.

BOBBY HULL

Bobby Hull

Bobby once said, "If I was to do it all over again, I wouldn't change a thing."

EASY FRUIT SALAD

1   (16-ounce) large carton whipped topping

1   (24-ounce) carton cottage cheese

1½ packages vanilla pudding mix

1   large can crushed pineapple, drained

2   regular cans Mandarin oranges, drained

1   regular bottle cherries, drained and reserved

Combine first 3 ingredients in a bowl, until mixed well. Add pineapple, oranges and cherries; mix together. Add cherry juice to give a little color, optional of course. Makes a whole big bunch. Enough to share. Best to make a day ahead. Keeps well.

Great as a refreshing side or even dessert.

DID YOU KNOW?

Hull ended his career, having played in 1063 NHL games, accumulating 610 goals, 560 assists, 1170 points, 640 penalty minutes, three Art Ross Trophies, two Hart Memorial Trophies, a Lady Byng Memorial Trophy, a Stanley Cup Championship, and adding 102 penalty minutes, 62 goals and 67 assists for 129 points in 119 playoff games. He played in 411 WHA games, scoring 303 goals, 335 assists and 638 points, adding 43 goals and 37 assists in 60 playoff games.

In 1978, he was made an Officer of the Order of Canada. Beside his Hall of Fame induction, Hull's #9 jersey has been retired both by the Blackhawks and the Jets (and is still honored by the Jets' successor team, the Phoenix Coyotes. When Bobby's son, Brett Hull joined the Coyotes, they unretired the number for Brett to wear during his brief stint there to honor his father.) Evander Kane, who wears number 9 for the current Winnipeg Jets franchise, sought and received Hull's permission to wear the number.

He currently serves as an ambassador for the Blackhawks' organization.

BOBBY HULL

EGGS BENEDICT WITH A TWIST

1   package McCormick's Béarnaise
      sauce
1   tablespoon butter
2   eggs
Fresh ground black pepper
1   English muffin, or sourdough bread
Boars Head® Pesto Parmesan ham, or
      Rosemary ham

Prepare Béarnaise sauce using ½ the butter and skim milk that is called for and follow package directions. When thickened, turn off heat. McCormick's Hollandaise is very lemony and very good, too.

Heat a skillet to medium heat; add butter until it melts. Add eggs (do not break the yolks) and fry until whites are done but yolks are not. Sprinkle with pepper. Toast English muffin or sourdough bread, purchased from the deli at your grocery store.

When ready to plate, layer the muffin or bread with thin sliced ham, flip eggs for 10 seconds and serve with the other side up. Cover with sauce and serve.

If you have trouble slicing muffins, substitute a nice slice of toasted bread.

JAM AND CREAM CHEESE CRÊPES

Premade crêpes
Soft cream cheese
Jam or jelly of your choice

Heat store bought large crêpes very lightly and be careful not to burn them. These can be done in a microwave. The goal is to get them warmed. Spread any favorite soft cream cheese on the crêpe lightly and then lightly spread jam or jelly over the cheese. Fold it all together, particularly the bottom to avoid dripping and wrap in wax paper to eat on the go.

EGGPLANT PARMESAN

1 eggplant
Olive oil
Eggbeaters
Italian bread crumbs
1 jar tomato basil sauce
Parmesan cheese, shredded or grated
Mozzarella, sliced

This is my favorite eggplant dish!
~Bob Griese

Cut off ends of a fresh plump purple eggplant and skin. Slice from the fat end and work to the top in ⅓-inch slices. Heat a large skillet to medium heat and cover the bottom with olive oil. Using 2 bowls, add eggbeaters to one and bread crumbs to the other. When the oil is warm, not too hot, dredge eggplant, starting with the fattest piece in the egg, then the bread crumbs. (Should fit 5 slices in the skillet at one time.) Place in skillet and cook until bottom is toasted, then flip and toast the other side. Add more oil as the patties absorb it even when you flip them if the pan is dry. Use a foil lasagna pan to make clean-up easy and cover the bottom with tomato basil sauce. You will know when the sections are done when your spatula edge indents. Remove and arrange in the pan. Repeat the process with the next fat sections. As the second batch cooks, sprinkle the first batch with Parmesan cheese and a full slice of mozzarella on each eggplant slice. If you find the eggplant is toasting too dark, reduce the heat to low. Repeat the process until you run out of eggplant. The ideal stack is 3. Finish the last one with Parmesan, mozzarella, and cover with the remaining sauce. Cover with foil and bake at 300 degrees for 30-40 minutes.

Can be made well in advance and stored as it is vegetarian and refrigerates well.
~Shay Griese

Keith Jackson

Keith is perhaps the most flattered broadcaster ever to sit in a booth. A versatile play-by-play man who has covered everything from baseball to boxing, his distinctive Southern twang is most associated with college football. He took the ABC announce booth every football Saturday for more than 30 years, during which his trademark "Whoa, Nellie!" became the stuff of legend.

HOT SMOKED SALMON

You need enough brine to cover your chunks of salmon. I almost always used at least a full bottle of Red wine. Red gives the whole process some character. I suggest a vinyl pan at least four inches deep...six won't hurt. After the wine...add some molasses...a cup. Then some sea salt...¼ cup ...½ cup brown sugar...a taste of honey if you like...make your own judgment on soy sauce but you need some ...like a little Tapatio Hot sauce, tablespoon might help. My final ingredients...garlic pepper or some black pepper...teaspoon followed by a full cup of a dry Sherry. I like Dry Sack!

Cover the meat with the brine...add water here if needed...give it 4-6 hours...smoking will require 3-4 hours...to get it flakey firm...it can be tested along the way with no damage.

When you judge it to be done...cool it...then peel the meat off the wire grills. The skin will stick. That will be your first batch...check the taste...adjust the brine to your taste and keep doing small batches until you have it just right...Then make smoked salmon till you drop...cuz everybody is gonna want some.

One of those flavor sealers is handy...you can seal it...and keep it a year or longer if you seal it.

If you chance to have a six or seven pound salmon...cut off the head and tail...open it up right down the middle of the underbelly. If you bought it at the market it will be cleaned...rescrape the outside to clean it...sprinkle some Blackened Redfish from Paul Prudhomme down the middle of the cavity...a touch of garlic salt...some ground black pepper...some fresh onion strips (Vidalia Sweet) is good... roll it up in sturdy aluminum foil...400 degrees...15 minutes is plenty. Slice the sourdough...pour the zinfandel...and have a hoot.

SPORTS BROADCASTING HALL OF FAME

Turi Ann and I bought a 'lil white house on Henry Point at the entrance to Pender Harbor in British Columbia located along the west coast of the Province and one of the prettiest settings we had ever seen. Surrounded by mountains high to send a lot of the bad weather bouncing over us. To the right of Henry Point was the confluence of the Malaspina Strait and the Georgia Strait and keeping order the big shoulders of the Mountains of Vancouver Island. Breathtaking to be sure! But...there was another element that added to this whole thing...the 'lil white house was right next to some of the best salt water fishing on the North American continent...!

My Norwegian Beauty had no trouble getting to the boat by sun up. And eight hours on the water was nothing because back in the 70's every kind of salmon was running around the area and in the deep rocky holes lots of tasty ling cod.

We had all the gear for the pursuit in short order including some Loomis mooching rods and a charge account for bait. We used live herring for mooching and drifting...never cared much for trolling...but sometimes you had to do it.

And you could load up the freezer in a week. Limits were quite liberal. So now we have caught all these salmon. Our youngest son Christopher at eleven years looked like a veteran after a month and within three months could put our 32 foot Uniflite on the dock slicker than me. What to do with this salmon. Some of the local folks suggested we can it or have it done. Keep it a long time that way.

Others said ...smoke it...two ways ...cold smoke it if you enjoy Lox...or hot smoke it after brining the meat. And thus began a wonderful adventure with fresh salmon. Hot Smoked Salmon!

We asked questions and listened hard and took notes as we got acquainted with the people in the community. And they were just as nice as possible I guess because we had proven we had come to stay and wanted to become adequated and responsible fishing citizens. Besides we paid cash for the 'lil white house!

The best answer we found for smoking fresh salmon was an aluminum box called the Little Chief made by a fishing tackle company in Hood River, Oregon.

The secret issue to me...at the start...was the "Brine"...that mixture that you soaked your meat in over nite...that provided most of the flavor.

Since we had the luxury of thick fillets from our salmon, coho and king primarily, I chose to cut into 2 squares. I would smoke just the pemmican stage which would provide a piece of salmon that would "flake" off perfectly for a small cracker. My favorite Triscuits. The electric smoker had 3 shelves and could handle about two pounds. The heat came from a heating pan that was located at the bottom of the smoker. And just under the small pan that held the chips that made the smoke. Alder wood is the art's historic chip...still is the essential basic flavor. You buy it...it's easier. And there are other choices. Apple is very popular but I like alder first followed by cherry and once in a while hickory.

One pan of chips is light...I almost always used two full and a half. Leave the skin on the chunks of meat...it will stick to the wire grill and peel off when it's finished.

Now to the rest of the story and it really comes near the beginning with the Brine.

SHAY'S PARTY SALMON

2 pounds fresh skinless salmon, spine removed

Coconut extract

Cherry extract

½ cup spiced rum

1 cup molasses

½ cup brown sugar

Honey, to taste

½ cup soy sauce

Garlic pepper or black pepper, to taste

Cut salmon head to tail in 1½-inch strips. In a bowl, add brine, coconut extract, cherry extract and spiced rum; mix well. Add molasses, brown sugar, honey and soy sauce. No need to add salt, soy sauce is salty enough. Add salmon strips and enough water if needed to cover salmon. Add garlic pepper or black pepper, to taste. If too sweet add more water and if too sour add more sugar. Cover and refrigerate 4-6 hours or overnight.

When ready to smoke salmon, allow 3-4 hours for cooking. Remove rack from your smoker. Place chips on the bottom pan according to smoker direction. Alder or Cherry wood is best. Start with the thickest salmon pieces and place them on the bottom rack and continue upwards until all salmon pieces are used, ending with the thinnest strips. Smoke for 3-4 hours, or until it is firm and flaky when tested.

Carefully remove rack from smoker and let salmon dry to warm; the drying process is vital. Can be served warm or cooled, and can be refrigerated up to several months.

The Little Chief is the best smoker I have ever seen and comes with all supplies needed and a wonderful cookbook. For more information go to www.littlechiefsmoker.net.

BLACK BEANS AND RICE

2　large green bell peppers

1　onion

Olive oil

1　cup white vinegar

¼　cup sugar

1-2 large cans black beans, may
　　　substitute with red

10　ounces saffron yellow rice

Onions, chopped for garnish

Chop green peppers and onion. Add enough olive oil to coat the bottom of a sauté pan and sauté peppers and onion. Add vinegar and sugar; stir until sugar dissolves. Add black beans or red if you prefer. Cover and simmer for 1-2 hours, checking to make sure you have enough liquid. Taste the liquid and adjust sugar or vinegar to your taste. The sugar offsets the vinegar and likewise, and water added settles the whole thing down. Keep simmering until the beans produce a black color to the liquid, similar to a light gravy. Meantime, cook rice according to package directions. When rice is ready, you can serve. Use a bowl and add a spoon of rice, then cover with bean mixture. Garnish with finely chopped onions.

This meal is great alone, or with barbequed meat and it's vegetarian so it stores and freezes very well.

~Shay Griese

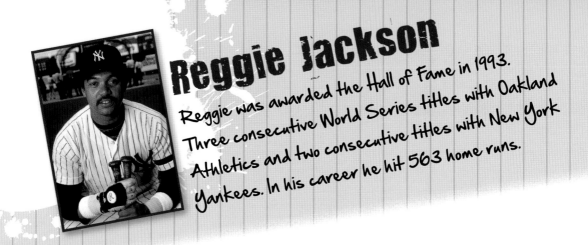

Reggie Jackson

Reggie was awarded the Hall of Fame in 1993. Three consecutive World Series titles with Oakland Athletics and two consecutive titles with New York Yankees. In his career he hit 563 home runs.

SMOOTHIE

1 rounded scoop whey protein powder

1 cup orange juice

½ cup strawberries

¼ cup blueberries

1 (6-ounce) yogurt, flavored if you like

½ cup ice

Mix all ingredients in a blender and process until smooth.

Optional: Substitute different fruits according to your taste.

DID YOU KNOW?

Reggie Jackson was born on May 18, 1946, in Wyncote, Pennsylvania. In high school he was a multi-sport star. Initially, he attended Arizona State on a football scholarship but switched to baseball during his freshmen year. Reggie replaced Rick Monday, (1st player ever taken in the inaugural Major League Draft) his sophomore year.

Over his 21 season career, Reggie played for 4 teams. He started his career in 1967 for the Kansas City Athletics who then moved to Oakland the next year. His tenure with the Athletics from '67-'75 led to 3 World Series championships in '72,'73, and '74. He played his 1976 season with the Baltimore Orioles. From 1977-1981 Reggie Jackson played for the New York Yankees and acquired his nickname there as "Mr. October." It was during Game 6 of the 1977 World Series where Reggie Jackson bombed 3 home runs in one game, becoming the 2nd person only to Babe Ruth to do so. Babe Ruth did it twice and Albert Pujols has since joined the club in the 2011 World Series. With the NYY, Reggie won 2 more World Series rings in 1977 and 1978. He played for the California Angels from '82-'86 and finally ended his career back in Oakland with the Athletics in 1987.

Along with his 5 World Series rings, Reggie won numerous other awards and trophies. He was a 14 time all-star, 2 time Silver Slugger Award winner, 2 time World Series MVP in 1973 and 1977, 1973 AL MVP winner, and the 1977 Babe Ruth Award recipient. He was also inducted into the Hall of Fame in 1993; the same year the New York Yankees retired his #44.

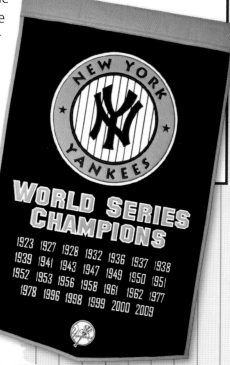

CARAMELIZED ONIONS.

1   medium onion of your choice
3   tablespoons oil or butter
Pinch salt
Pinch pepper, optional
Pinch sugar, optional

Slice the top and bottom off of onion; remove outer layer. Cut onion in half from top to bottom.

Place onion halves, flat side down on a cutting board. Slice onion into half-rings, ⅛ to ¼-inch thick.

Heat oil in a large skillet or saucepan over medium-high heat. If using butter be careful not to burn. When the oil begins to ripple, it is hot enough.

Add onions, stirring until they are coated with the oil. Add salt, pepper, and sugar, if using. Continue to stir the onions until the onions have begun to stick to the bottom of the pan and turn dark in color. This is okay—it's what should happen. If the onions are sticking too much, add a very small amount of water, broth or wine to the pan and stir vigorously; this is called "deglazing". Continue this process until the onions have reached the color, flavor and texture you desire.

Caramelizing onions brings out their amazing natural flavor. They're terrific on sandwiches and pizzas, over pastas, in soups, on meat, fish, and egg dishes, or adorning appetizer platters.

You can caramelize any type of onion. Some just caramelize more quickly than others. It all depends on their sugar content.

RED ONION SIDE DISH

3   red onions, thinly sliced and halved
Apple cider vinegar
3   tablespoons sugar
Red wine

In a covered saucepan, add onions, vinegar, sugar, and red wine. Simmer covered over low heat for 1 hour. Test flavor adding more sugar or liquid to taste. When onions are fully cooked (this could take 2-3 hours) and limp; add liquid as needed. Remove the lid and boil off the liquid. Goal is for sweet and sour mild onions that are great in salads or as a side for any meat.

Remember, sugar offsets sour, so add according to your desired taste but don't scrimp on the sugar as the onions should be caramelized.
~Shay Griese

CHICKEN PARMESAN

Chicken breast fillets (Tyson® fully
     cooked frozen fillets can be used)
Olive oil, for frying
Tomato basil sauce, your choice
Mozzarella cheese, sliced

In a skillet, cook chicken breast very slowly in a small amount of olive oil until light brown and cooked through. Pour tomato basil sauce of your choice to cover chicken. When sauce is warm, top with slices of mozzarella cheese and serve.

CREAMED SPINACH

1 large bag chopped frozen spinach

1 (8-ounce) package cream cheese, regular, light or fat free

Sea salt, to taste

1 tablespoon butter

Garlic, optional

Thaw spinach in a colander so it will drain and press with your hand, once thawed, to remove any additional water. In a large skillet, warm the spinach; add cream cheese, sea salt, butter, and garlic if using. Heat over medium heat, mixing ingredients all together and serve.

BEEF GOULASH

⅓ cup extra-virgin olive oil

2-3 white onions, peeled and chopped

2½ pounds boned, trimmed beef round,
   cut in 1-inch chunks

2 teaspoons salt

2 teaspoons paprika

1 teaspoon dried oregano

Sprinkle rosemary

3 cups bouillon, low sodium

4 tablespoons tomato paste

Instant roux

Sour cream

In a sauté pan over medium heat, add oil and onions. Sauté until onions are tender. Add beef, salt, paprika, oregano, and rosemary; sauté until lightly brown. In a crock-pot on medium to medium low heat, add beef mixture, bouillon, tomato paste and instant roux. Cook until meat is fork tender. Serve topped with a dollop of sour cream.

~Margie Engle

Margie Engle and Indigo, commissioned work displayed
in the Griese home by Lila Blakesley.

Ron Jaworski

Ron finished his 17-season career with 2,187 completions on 4,117 attempts for 28,190 yards, 179 touchdowns, and 164 interceptions. He also rushed for 859 yards and 16 touchdowns. He previously held the record for most consecutive starts by a quarterback with 116 having since been surpassed by Brett Favre and Peyton Manning. His 170 regular season touchdowns with the Philadelphia Eagles were the most in franchise history until he was surpassed by Donovan McNabb on September 21, 2008, 22 years after Jaworski left Philadelphia.

OYSTER PIE

Butter

Saltine crackers

1   large can oysters

Salt and pepper, to taste

16   ounces half & half

Generously butter the bottom and sides of a pie pan. Mash saltine crackers and place a layer on bottom of pie pan. Place a layer of oysters with salt and pepper. Place 4-5 dabs of butter on top of oysters.

Make another layer of crackers, oysters, salt, pepper, and butter, ending with a layer of crackers.

Pour half & half almost to the top of the pan. Bake at 400 degrees for 20-25 minutes.

Enjoy!

DID YOU KNOW?

Ron Jaworski was born on March 23, 1951, in Lackawanna, New York. After turning down a baseball contract with the St. Louis Cardinals, Ron took his talents to Youngstown State where he played from 1970-1973.

He began his professional career with the St. Louis Rams in 1973-1977. In the spring of 1977, Jaworski was traded by the Rams to the Philadelphia Eagles. He received his biggest notoriety and fame from his years with the Philadelphia Eagles from 1977-1986.

In 1979, he received a medal from Pope John Paul II for his Polish Ancestry. In 1980, he received Pro Bowl honors and in 1985 was the recipient of the Ed Block Courage Award.

Jaworski was nicknamed "Jaws" by Philadelphia 76ers player (and now coach) Doug Collins prior to the 1981 Super Bowl.

He ended his career with the Miami Dolphins and finally the Kansas City Chiefs in 1989. Presently, he along with Mike Tirico and Jon Gruden share Monday Night Football duties together.

SHAY'S SIGNATURE RIB RECIPE

2   slabs babyback ribs

Water

Barbecue sauce, to taste
     (any barbecue sauce will work)

Preheat oven to 300 degrees. Cut 2 slabs of ribs in half. Place in large aluminum pan, bone down, and rub meat side with the sauce generously. Fill pan with water until half full. Seal tightly with aluminum foil. Place in oven and cook for 2 hours.

Remove from oven and drain the liquids; repeat entire process. Cover and return to oven for 2 hours at 275 degrees.

John Madden

1976 Super Bowl XI winning head coach with Oakland Raiders. In 2006, he was inducted into the Pro Football Hall of Fame in recognition of his coaching career. CBS, Fox broadcaster, ABC's Monday Night Football commentator, and his last role was for NBC Sunday Night Football.

JOHN MADDEN'S LAMB STEW

Serves 12-15

7   pounds stewing lamb, cubed
1   cup water
1   pound carrots, peeled, cut into
       1-inch sections
2   yellow onions, diced
1   quart tomato sauce
1   quart beer
2   cups white wine
1   garlic clove
½   cup fresh parsley
     Garlic powder, to taste
     Seasoning salt, to taste
     Salt, to taste
     Black pepper or Tabasco® sauce,
       to taste

Place lamb in a large covered pot (preferably a Dutch oven). Brown meat slightly to render fat. Add water and bring to a boil. Stir. Keep heat high until meat is browned.

Drain excess fat, leaving small amount for flavor.

Add remaining ingredients, except seasonings. Stir well.

Add seasonings in small amounts. Cover; bring to boil. Stir. Boil 15 minutes more.

Reduce heat to low. Stir completely. Season to taste.

Simmer 1½ hours, stirring every 15 minutes. Check carrot tenderness. Continue seasoning to taste.

Stew is done when carrots are tender. Remove from heat. Let stand 10 minutes. Skim fat.

VIRGINIA MADDEN'S BREAD PUDDING

Makes 2 (9x13-inch) pans

2   loaves bread
½   gallon whole milk
8   eggs
2-3 cups granulated sugar
3   tablespoons vanilla
2-3 cups raisins or other fruit
3   sticks real butter
2   cups powdered sugar
½-1 cup cheap whiskey

Preheat oven to 325 degrees. Cut bread into 1-inch squares and place in a bowl. Pour milk over bread and let stand at least 1-2 hours.

In another bowl, beat 5-6 eggs with granulated sugar and vanilla. Pour into bowl with bread. Add raisins or fruit. Pour into 2 oil-sprayed pans. Bake 1 hour. Let cool. While cooling, make sauce.

Heat butter over low heat. Mix in powdered sugar. Stir over low heat until sugar is dissolved. Remove from heat and let cool. Beat remaining eggs and whisk into the sauce. Now the good part: add whiskey and mix well. Pour sauce over pudding, using a fork to get the sauce into entire pudding.

Great with ice cream, coffee or whatever. Enjoy!

JOHN MADDEN

69

GRIESE SHOTS

70

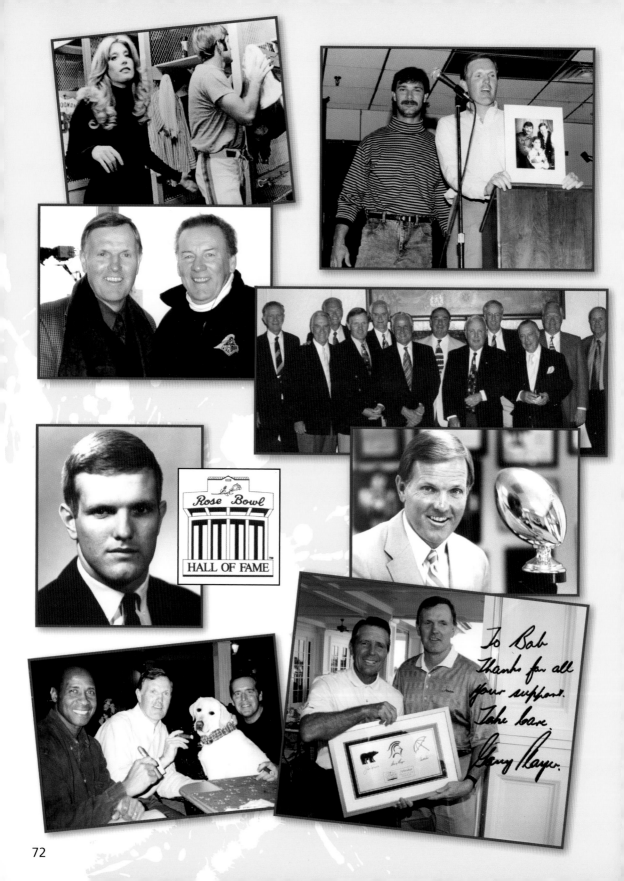

Rose Bowl
HALL OF FAME

To Bob
Thanks for all
your support.
Take care.
Gary Player.

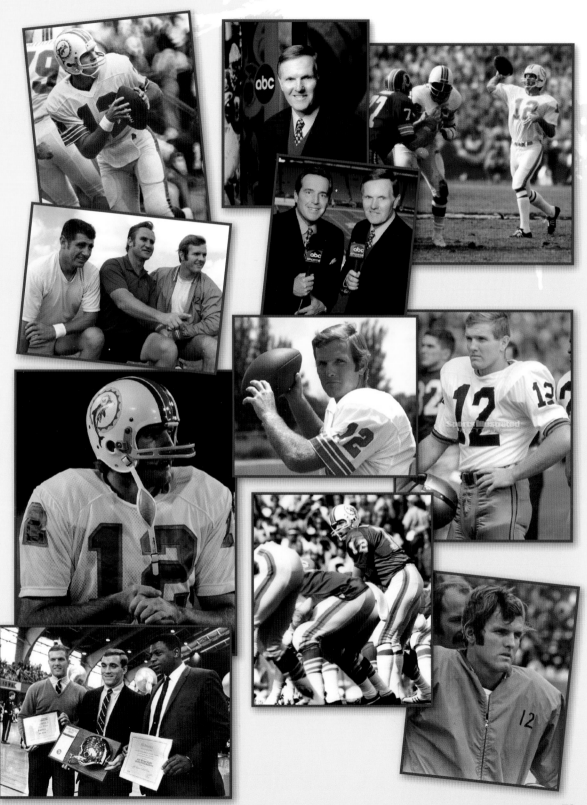

CORN OFF THE COB WITH PEPPERS AND ONIONS

4-5 ears of corn
Onion, finely chopped
Red bell peppers
Green bell peppers
Vegetable oil
Salt and pepper, to taste

Cut fresh corn off the cob into a bowl and set aside. In a separate bowl, finely chop onion, red and green bell peppers. In a skillet, heat vegetable oil over medium heat. Add onion and peppers and sauté for about 10 minutes. Add fresh corn kernels and continue to sauté until corn is crispy but warmed. Salt and pepper to taste. Serve.

Place a small cutting board that will fit inside a brownie pan and hold the corn on end and with a sharp knife strip the kernels. This will keep them from flying all over the place.

-Shay Griese

CHINESE NOODLES

2-3 packages pork shoulder,
    ¾-inch thick

Vegetable or canola oil

Soy sauce, low sodium

2-3 hard-boiled eggs

Angel hair pasta, snapped in half

Chives, green part only

Cut pork off the bone and trim the meat of excess fat; then cut meat into strips about the size of your pinky finger. In a skillet, heat oil on medium heat. Add strips of meat and cook, turning meat around to brown on all sides. Sprinkle liberally with soy sauce. At the same time you are cooking the pork, add enough water to a stockpot to hard boil eggs. Remove eggs, add pasta, and cook until done. Drain pasta well, adding dashes of soy sauce and oil so it's not sticky and toss in the colander. Spread pasta in a shallow salad dish and top with pork, egg and then snips of the green part of chives to garnish.

Before Bob and I were married 18 years ago I rented a great converted apartment for years on Miami Beach from Cyd and Dave Penny who lived in their main house. Cyd grew up in Oregon and the family finances were limited. Her mother would make this dish and taught Cyd the recipe. Certainly, the three of us were all fortunate financially with great jobs in Miami but the recipe stuck with us. It is so inexpensive and delicious and Cyd hooked me on it. To this day I keep pork shoulder in the freezer because you never know when you get a craving for Chinese Noodles.

~Shay Griese, Ala Cyd Penny

Dan Marino

Dan became the first player ever to pass for 5,000 yards in a single season, finishing with a remarkable 5,084 yards. Marino was named first- or second-team All-Pro eight times and earned All-AFC honors six times. Elected to Pro Football Hall of Fame on February 5, 2005, and enshrined on August 7, 2005.

BOLOGNESE SAUCE

Makes 9 cups

2 tablespoons olive oil

1½ pounds each ground beef and pork

Kosher salt and pepper, to taste

4 ounces pancetta, cut into ½-inch dice

1 yellow onion, finely diced

2 carrots, peeled and finely diced

1 celery stalk, finely diced

5 garlic cloves, minced

½ cup tomato paste

1 cup dry red wine

1 cup milk

2 (28-ounce) cans diced tomatoes passed through a food mill

3 bay leaves

1 Parmigiano-Reggiano cheese rind

1 pound tagliatelle, cooked

In stovetop-safe insert of slow cooker, over medium-high heat, warm 1 tablespoon of the olive oil. Cook beef, pork, salt, and pepper for 12 minutes. Drain on paper towels. Cook pancetta 7 minutes. Drain on paper towels.

Reduce heat to medium; warm remaining oil. Cook onion, carrots, and celery 8 minutes. Add garlic; cook 1 minute. Add tomato paste; cook 2 minutes. Add wine; simmer 5 minutes. Add meats, pancetta, milk, tomatoes, bay leaves, cheese, salt, and pepper. Bring to simmer. Remove from stovetop and place inside on slow cooker base. Cover and cook on high 3½ hours. Discard bay leaves and rind. Toss pasta with 3 cups sauce; reserve remaining sauce.

DID YOU KNOW?

Dan Marino was born on September 15, 1961, in Pittsburgh, Pennsylvania. He decided to stay in his home state, like Ditka, and attend Pittsburgh. He led the Pittsburgh Panthers from 1979-1982 with an electric victory over the Georgia Bulldogs during the 1982 season. Georgia was led by a spectacular freshmen running back, Hershel Walker.

Marino was drafted and played his entire career with the Miami Dolphins from 1983-1999. Over his professional career Marino amassed a war chest of records and awards. He was a 9 time Pro Bowler, the NFL MVP in 1984, recipient of the 1998 Walter Payton Man of the Year, 1984 Offensive Player of the Year, and holds over 31 Miami Dolphins records. At one point, Dan Marino held or was tied for over 40 NFL records. He received induction into the College Football Hall of Fame in 2003 and the Pro football Hall of Fame in 2005. The Dolphins retired his 'lucky' #13 jersey in 2000.

On Sunday, September 17, 2000, at halftime of the Dolphins-Baltimore Ravens game at Pro Player Stadium, Dan Marino's jersey #13 was retired. The only other Dolphins jersey number retired at the time was Bob Griese's #12. Since then #39, Larry Csonka, has been retired as well. Marino joined the Dolphins Honor Roll the same day. In a year of accolades from the franchise he led for many years, the Dolphins also installed a life-size bronze statue of Marino at Pro Player Stadium (now Sun Life Stadium) and renamed Stadium Street, Dan Marino Boulevard.

Marino is currently an analyst for CBS's Sunday pregame show *The NFL Today*. He was formerly a studio analyst on HBO's *Inside the NFL*.

FRESH SALAD WITH GOAT CHEESE MEDALLIONS

SALAD

Lettuce of your choice, other than romaine, I prefer bagged butter lettuce

Endive

Radicchio

Green onion

Cherry tomatoes, halved

DRESSING

1   part red wine vinegar, or lemon juice

2   parts olive oil

Sea salt and pepper, to taste

Grainy mustard

Honey

1   log goat cheese, sliced

Seasoned bread crumbs

Chop lettuce and set aside. Chop endive, radicchio, and green onion. Add to lettuce and toss with tomato halves.

To Make Dressing: Whisk together in a bowl, vinegar, or lemon juice, olive oil, sea salt, pepper, mustard, and honey. Refrigerate salad and dressing. Take the log of goat cheese and slice into medallions, patting them tightly. Pour seasoned breadcrumbs in a bowl and bread the medallions. Heat a skillet to medium, adding a light coating of olive oil. Add medallions, toasting one side then the other. Whisk salad dressing again and toss into the salad. Garnish with medallions.

If the medallions seem too soft due to the handling, just put them in the freezer for 10-15 minutes. Otherwise, they can melt a little while frying, but that's not all that bad either.

~Shay Griese

78

ROASTED ASPARAGUS, TOMATO, BUFFALO MOZZARELLA SALAD

Heirloom tomatoes
1   large ball buffalo mozzarella
Asparagus cut in 4-inch lengths
Olive oil
Fresh basil, finely chopped
Balsamic vinegar
Mayonnaise
Salt and pepper, to taste

Slice tomatoes and mozzarella in matching widths, about ¼-inch thick. Try to find heirlooms in season in various colors. Break asparagus at the weak spot which will give you about 4-inch lengths. Discard the stalk.

In a skillet, cook asparagus on medium heat in olive oil until fork tender. On a long, thin platter arrange tomatoes and cheese alternately down the length or diagonally. Then frame with cooked asparagus. Sprinkle with basil. In a separate bowl add vinegar, olive oil, mayonnaise, salt and pepper; whisk together and drizzle over basil.

Wine Paring: A White Zinfandel will taste wonderful with this dish.

Try never to refrigerate tomatoes; it strips their flavor.   ~Shay Griese

Don Mattingly

Don is a former Major League baseball first baseman and current manager of the Los Angeles Dodgers. Nicknamed "The Hit Man" and "Donnie Baseball", he played his entire 14-year baseball career for the New York Yankees (1982-1995). After his playing career, he also served as a hitting coach for the Yankees and Dodgers prior to taking on his current position as manager of the Dodgers.

BIRD NEST

1   slice bread
     Butter
1   egg

Butter both sides of bread slice. Tear a hole in the bread about the size of the yolk of an egg. Place bread slice in a skillet and brown lightly. Add egg into the hole, lightly cook on that side and then flip. Brown bread on the other side as the egg cooks. The yolk should be like a sunny side up egg.

Don Mattingly was born on September 9, 1951, in Evansville, Indiana. A graduate of Memorial High School in Evansville, Indiana in 1979, he led the Tigers to a state record 59 straight victories through the 1978-79 seasons. In 1978 the Tigers were crowned State Champions and were State Runners-up in 1979.

Don considered the college ranks after high school but after being drafted by the Yankees he decided otherwise. Don played for the New York Yankees from 1982-1995. He served as their captain during the 1991-1995 seasons and retained the nicknames "The Hit Man" and "Donnie Baseball." He was a 6 time all-star, a 9 time Gold Glover, received 3 Silver Slugger awards, and set a MLB record with 6 grand slams in one season. He received the 1985 AL MVP as a Yankee, tied the AL record for 10 consecutive games with an extra base hit, and tied a MLB record with 8 homeruns in 8 consecutive games. The New York Yankees retired "Donnie Baseball's" #23 jersey in 1997.

Today, Don Mattingly manages the LA Dodgers.

DON MATTINGLY

KITCHEN SINK SALAD

SALAD

Radicchio

Endive

Mild onion

Red cabbage

Fresh spinach

Whole kernel corn, cut off
the cob is best

1   can hearts of palm

1   can artichoke hearts

Sliced sandwich ham, cubed

Cherry tomatoes, halved

Shredded sharp Cheddar cheese

5   hard-boiled eggs, chopped

Pickled beet, sliced

Roasted red pepper

1   can Mandarin oranges

Crumbled blue cheese or Gorgonzola

DRESSING

Marzetti or dressing of your choice

SALAD

In a large salad bowl, chop radicchio, endive, onion, cabbage, and spinach in bite-size pieces. Add corn, hearts of palm, and artichoke hearts. Add sliced ham, then toss. Arrange tomatoes around the rim of the bowl on top of lettuce. Sprinkle with Cheddar cheese and chopped eggs. Add beets, red peppers, and then Mandarin oranges. Top with crumbled blue cheese or Gorgonzola.

DRESSING

Dressings can vary depending on your taste. Marzetti makes wonderful veggie dips in white tubs; when cut with balsamic or red wine vinegar it makes a great salad dressing. I favor the blue cheese. The over-the-top best salad dressing for this recipe (or any other salad) comes from Hartville Kitchen in Hartville, Ohio (see page 149). Their Sweet and Sour dressing is without question the best bottled salad dressing I have ever eaten and it comes light and fat-free, but the others are fantastic too. Anyway, on this salad it's your kitchen sink salad dressing choice!

This salad is all about color and presentation but the taste combination is not boring so chop everything you have in your crisper into bite-size pieces!

~Shay Griese

TOMATO MOZZARELLA SALAD

1 Buffalo mozzarella ball, cut
   into bite-size pieces

Heirloom tomatoes or cherry tomatoes,
   halved (assorted colors if possible)

English cucumber

Balsamic vinegar

Olive oil

Mild onions

Fresh basil

Parsley

Blue cheese

In a large mixing bowl, add all the ingredients and toss.

Jack Nicklaus

Jack, nicknamed "The Golden Bear", is an American professional golfer. He won 18 career major championships on the PGA Tour over a span of 25 years and is widely regarded as one of the greatest professional golfers of all time. In addition to his 18 Majors, he was runner-up a record 19 times, and placed 3rd an additional 9 times. Nicklaus did not play that many tournaments because he wanted to focus on the Majors, but is still second on the PGA-tournament winning list, with 73 victories.

RED VELVET CAKE

2½ cups all-purpose flour
1   tablespoon baking soda
1   tablespoon cocoa powder
1½ cups vegetable oil
2   eggs
½ bottle red food coloring
1½ cups sugar
1   tablespoon vinegar
1   tablespoon vanilla
1   cup buttermilk

CREAM CHEESE FROSTING
1   (8-ounce) package cream cheese, softened
1   box 10x confectioners' sugar
1   stick butter, softened
1   teaspoon vanilla

Preheat oven to 350 degrees. Grease and flour 3 (8-inch) round cake pans.

In a bowl, sift together flour, baking soda, and cocoa; set aside. In a separate bowl, beat together oil, eggs, food coloring, sugar, vinegar, and vanilla. Add flour mixture and buttermilk alternately to sugar mixture. Pour into prepared cake pans. Bake for 15-20 minutes.

While cake is cooling prepare Cream Cheese Frosting.

In a large bowl, mix cream cheese, sugar, and butter on low speed until incorporated. Increase the speed to high, and mix until light and fluffy, about 5 minutes.

Add vanilla and mix until fluffy. Store in refrigerator until somewhat stiff. Spread between layers and on top of cake.

DID YOU KNOW?

Jack Nicklaus was born on January 21, 1940, in Columbus, Ohio. Jack attended and was later granted an honorary Doctorate from The Ohio State University in 1972. He turned Pro in 1962 and took home Rookie of the Year honors. He is regarded as the greatest golf player ever, holding the PGA record with 18 major championships. He is a 6 time Masters, 4 time U.S. Open champion, 3 time British Open Champion, and 5 time PGA champion. He has battled legendary opponents with names the likes of Ben Hogan, Sam Snead, Gary Player, Arnold Palmer, and Johnny Miller. Nicklaus, along with Gene Sarazen, Ben Hogan, Gary Player, and Tiger Woods, are the only players to win four major championships, now known as the Career Slam. Over his historic career, Nicklaus received 5 PGA player of the Year awards, the '75 Bobby Jones award, 2000 Payne Stewart Award, and finally in 2008 the PGA tour lifetime achievement award. In 1974, The World Golf Hall of Fame inducted Nicklaus into its list of greats.

In the Masters he holds the record for most eagles with 24, most birdies with 506, most cuts made with 37, most top-10 finishes with 22, most top-five finishes with 15, runner-up a record four times and holds the record for most wins with six which is two more than Arnold Palmer and Tiger Woods.

In the U.S. Open, he holds the record with Willie Anderson, Bobby Jones and Ben Hogan for most wins at the U.S Open with four, 18 top-10 finishes, 11 top-five finishes, and four runner-up finishes.

In the British Open, he won three times, runner-up a record seven times, a record 16 top-five finishes, and finally a record 18 top-10 finishes.

In the PGA Championship, Nicklaus holds the record with Walter Hagen for most wins with 5. He was runner-up four times, most top-five finishes with 14, and for most top-10 finishes with 15. He is first in major runner-up finishes as well with an astonishing 19.

After retiring from golf, Nicklaus has proven himself to be a world renown golf designer and presently has a museum back home in Columbus, Ohio filled with memorabilia and other interesting pieces from his golfing days.

JACK NICKLAUS

PENNE PASTA WITH SHRIMP AND PEAS

1   package penne pasta
1   small bag cooked frozen shrimp
½   cup frozen peas
Olive oil
Clove garlic, chopped
Roasted red peppers
Parmesan cheese
1   jar tomato sauce
Fresh basil, chopped
Heavy cream

Cook pasta according to package directions. Thaw cooked frozen shrimp, remove the tails and place in a tall-sided skillet. Place frozen peas in the skillet with olive oil and cook on medium heat. Add fresh chopped garlic and rough chopped roasted red peppers. Drain pasta. Transfer pasta and shrimp mixture to a large serving bowl and toss in liberal amount of Parmesan cheese, 2-3 ounces of tomato sauce, basil and heavy cream. Garnish with chopped basil and Parmesan cheese. Serve.

CHICKEN WITH CAPERS AND PORT WINE SAUCE

Fully cooked Tyson® breaded chicken breast fillets

Equal parts peanut oil or 1 package instant roux sauce mix

Chicken or beef stock, low sodium

Port wine, Sherry or white wine, to taste

Caper and lemon wedges, for garnish

In a skillet, heat enough oil to coat the bottom to medium heat. Fry fillets on both sides till crispy. Remove and keep warm in foil.

To Make Sauce: If using instant roux sauce mix, follow package directions. Add wine to taste. Pour over chicken and sprinkle with capers and garnish with lemon wedges.

CHICKEN WITH MUSHROOMS AND RED WINE SAUCE

Prepare chicken the same as the Chicken with Capers. The sauce is the same basic sauce with sautéed mushrooms in butter, garlic, red wine or Marsala wine for a sweeter taste and the roux.

Joe Paterno

Joe's coaching portfolio includes two National Championships (1982, 1986); five undefeated, untied teams; 23 finishes in the Top 10 of the national rankings; an unprecedented five AFCA Coach-of-the-Year plaques. Paterno is the only coach to win the four traditional New Year's Day bowl games — the Rose, Sugar, Cotton and Orange Bowls.

SUE'S SALSA

Makes 6 pints

11   ripe tomatoes, peeled and chopped
½   cup kosher salt
1   cup coarsely chopped celery
1   cup coarsely chopped onion
3   sweet green peppers, coarsely
      chopped and seeded
4   sweet red peppers, coarsely
      chopped and seeded
6   jalapeño peppers, chopped
⅔   cup granulated sugar
¼   cup brown sugar
½   cup cider vinegar
¼   cup lime juice
8   ounces tomato paste
8   ounces chopped
      green chiles, drained

In a glass bowl (do not use metal) mix tomatoes with salt. Cover and let stand overnight. Drain well but do not rinse. In enamel kettle, add tomatoes, celery, onion, peppers, and jalapeños (using seeds if hot salsa is preferred), sugars, vinegar, lime juice, tomato paste, and drained chopped green chiles. Bring to a slow boil and cook 15 minutes, stirring frequently. Ladle into hot sterilized jars; seal and process in hot water bath for 20 minutes.

Joe Paterno was born on December 21, 1926, in Brooklyn, New York and died on January 22, 2012, in College Station. Before heading off to Brown University, Joe Paterno served in the Army for one year. As a player for Brown during '46-'49 he played as a Quarterback and Defensive Back. He is still tied for 1st place for career interceptions at Brown alongside Greg Parker. In 1950, he graduated from Brown University and rather than continue schooling to become a lawyer, he took up the assistant coaching position for Penn State in 1950. From 1950-1965 he served as an assistant coach before taking the reins as Head Coach in 1965. During his tenure, he was given the nickname, "JoePa," which he became synonymous for until his death. The years of 1965-2011 JoePa implanted himself in College Football history. He holds the record for Most Division 1-A/FBS wins with 409 and most bowl victories with 24. He is the proud recipient of the 1986 Paul "Bear" Bryant award, 2 time Bobby Dodd award winner, 2 time national champion in 1982 and '86, 2005 Sportsman of the Year, and 2011 Gerald R. Ford award winner. To his family, friends, and colleagues he was known as an Educator, Coach, and Humanitarian.

JOE
PATERNO

ZUCCHINI RIPIENI   *Stuffed Zucchini Baked in Tomato Sauce*

Serves 4 to 6

1½ cups tomato sauce, homemade or canned

4 medium-sized zucchini, scrubbed but not peeled

¼ cup olive oil

½ cup finely chopped onions

½ teaspoon finely chopped garlic

½ pound ground beef chuck

1 egg, lightly beaten

2 ounces finely chopped prosciutto (about ¼ cup), optional

½ cup fresh white bread crumbs (from French or Italian bread)

6 tablespoons freshly grated imported Parmesan cheese

½ teaspoon dried oregano, crumbled

1 teaspoon salt

¼ teaspoon freshly ground black pepper

Prepare the tomato sauce if using homemade. Preheat the oven to 375 degrees. Cut zucchini in half lengthwise and spoon out most of the pulp, leaving hollow boat like shells about ¼-inch thick. Set shells aside and chop pulp coarsely. Heat 3 tablespoons of olive oil in a heavy 8- to 10-inch skillet; add onions and cook over moderate heat for 8 to 10 minutes, or until they are soft and lightly colored. Add zucchini pulp and garlic; cook for about 5 minutes longer, stirring frequently. With a rubber spatula scrape the entire contents of the skillet into a large sieve set over a mixing bowl and let them drain.

Meanwhile heat a tablespoon of the oil in the skillet; add ground beef and brown it over moderate heat, stirring almost constantly with a large fork to break up any lumps. Scrape the beef into another sieve set over a bowl and let it drain.

Now, in a large mixing bowl, combine the drained vegetables and meat. Add lightly beaten egg, prosciutto, bread crumbs, 2 teaspoons of the grated cheese, oregano, salt, and pepper to taste. Spoon this stuffing into the hollowed zucchini shells, mounding the top slightly. To bake zucchini, use a 12x16-inch shallow baking dish into which 1½ cups tomato sauce have been poured. Then carefully arrange the stuffed zucchini on the sauce. Sprinkle their tops with ¼ cup cheese; dribble a few drops olive oil over them and cover the dish tightly with aluminum foil. Bring the sauce to a simmer on top of the stove, then transfer the dish to the middle of the oven and bake zucchini for 30 minutes, removing the foil after 20 minutes so that the tops of zucchini can brown lightly. Serve directly from the baking dish.

Joe Paterno

Joe has passionately served the Penn State football program and the university with principle, distinction and success with honor since matriculating to State College in 1950. After 16 years as an assistant coach, he was rewarded in 1966 with the head coaching responsibilities surrendered by the retiring Rip Engle, his college coach at Brown who appointed him to the Penn State staff in 1950 as a brash 23-year old.

Margie Engle

Margie's hometown is in Wellington, Florida. She may be small but she is gutsy, determined and relentless—are just a few words that can describe one of the US' most successful jumping riders of all time. Her love for riding and horse is evident in so many firsts and records in her career.

Indigo with the Miami Dolphin emblem on his saddle pad.

DID YOU KNOW?

To name a few of her records and careers, Margie was a part of the U.S. Silver medal team at the 2006 WEG. In 2008, she won the Bob Thomas Grand Prix of Florida. She enjoyed a successful 2009 campaign, placing sixth in the HITS Grand Prix at HITS.

Margie and her team traveled to Kentucky, where she placed at the Kentucky Horse Park in the KHJA Grand Prix, Haygard Medical Institute Grand Prix and the Prix De Penn National Grand Prix which also served as a World Cup qualifier.

Over the years she has suffered injuries, with a broken hip in 2004, but just a short 3 months later she was riding Hidden Creeks' Perin and beat a field of 26 entries. Now that is determination!

She has over 190 Grand Prix wins and has been named AGA Rider of the Year ten times, has more that 20 winning National Cup teams, and was the 1991 AHSA Equestrian of the Year.

In 1992 and 1993, Margie was named the Rolex/National Grand Prix League Rider of the Year. In 1999, she won a silver medal at the Pan American Games in Winnipeg, Canada. At the 2000 Olympic Games in Sydney, Australia, she was the highest placed woman and the highest placed U.S. rider in the individual competition. In 2007, she won RV Sales of Broward Grand Prix at HITS Saugerties.

In 2010, Margie had another successful year on a number of different horses at WEF. She claimed top prize in Round II of the WEF Challenge Cup.

Indigo, co-owned by Margie Engle, Bob & Shay Griese, and Mike Powlaski (Graffitos Restaurant, Wellington, FL.), were victorious in the 2012 FEI World Cup Qualifier Grand Prix the fastest of two clear round in an eleven horse jump-off. As of April 2012, Indigo is #1 in the nation.

CROCKPOT TURKEY

1   (3 pound) Butterball® boneless
    turkey breast
1   can whole cranberry sauce
1   can Mandarin oranges

Thaw turkey breast in warm water until you can feel the outside getting slightly soft. Carefully remove the gravy package, being careful not to puncture the packet. Remove plastic encasing from turkey breast and place breast in crockpot with a little bouillon or water. Cover. Set crockpot on low for 5 hours.

In a small saucepan, prepare gravy according to package directions.

Serve with whole cranberry sauce mixed with Mandarin oranges.

CHICKEN POT PIE

1 prepared rotisserie chicken
    (2 if they are small)

1-2 large cans low sodium mushroom
    soup

½ cup low sodium chicken or beef
    bouillon

1 cup mixed vegetables

Frozen buttermilk biscuits

Strip chicken from bones and place meat in a crockpot. Add mushroom soup and make sure you have another one just in case. Add chicken or beef bouillon, and a cup or more frozen mixed vegetables. Thaw frozen biscuits and when thawed bake until just golden. Serve the mixture in bowls with the biscuits halved and placed on top.

The easiest recipe ever! If you are in a hurry, cooking time in the oven should be 20–25 minutes in a covered Dutch oven at 350 degrees but I precook the veggies to insure the green beans aren't hard. If you want to rush set the crockpot on high heat and place veggies in first with the bouillon and wait until the beans are fork tender until you add the chicken and soup. Once you add the chicken and soup switch heat to low. If you are not in a rush, the crockpot on low is best and it can sit for hours.

~Shay Griese

Gale Sayers

Sayers, Kansas All-American. Led NFL rushers, 1966. 1969 named all-time NFL halfback. Player of Game in three pro bowls. NFL lifetime kickoff return leader. Gale Sayers was nicknamed the "Kansas Comet" years before he knew he would leave small towns in the heartland for the bright lights of Chicago. But after his sparkling, brief career, the nickname seemed much more fitting.

EASY HOMEMADE MACARONI AND CHEESE

Makes about 6 (1 cup) servings

1½ cups uncooked elbow macaroni
½ stick butter
3 tablespoons all-purpose flour
1½ teaspoons dried mustard
¾ teaspoon onion powder
3 cups 2% milk
3 cups cubed American cheese
½ cup crushed cornflakes

Preheat oven to 350 degrees.

Cook macaroni according to package directions and drain.

Melt butter in a 3-quart saucepan until sizzling. Stir in flour, dried mustard, and onion powder. Add milk, stirring constantly until mixture boils and thickens, about 5 to 7 minutes.

Reduce heat to low; stir in cheese. Cook until cheese is melted. Add cooked macaroni, mix well and pour into greased casserole dish. Sprinkle cornflakes on top. Bake in preheated oven for 30 to 35 minutes.

Sayers was born in rural Kansas, and his family migrated to Omaha, NE, before his high school years. After a star-studded four years at Omaha Central, Sayers turned down offers from several other colleges to play at the University of Kansas. There in Lawrence, the running back would be named an all-American player twice, and finished with 2,675 yards rushing.

In the 1965 draft, Sayers was not only picked by the Bears with their fourth selection of the first round, but also selected in the first round by the Kansas City Chiefs of the AFL. Sayers wasn't even the Bears' first selection that season: they also held the third pick, which they used on Illinois linebacker Dick Butkus. Sayers ended up turning down more money with the Chiefs to play with the established NFL.

The young phenom would go on to score 22 touchdowns: 14 rushing, 6 receiving and 2 on returns, and compile a combined 1,347 rushing and receiving yards.

The rookie was voted the NFL's Offensive Rookie of the Year, and set an NFL record with his 22 total touchdowns.

The following year, 1966, proved to be Sayers' best. He rushed for 1,231 yards and caught passes for another 447.

In 1977, Gale Sayers became the youngest player ever inducted into the Pro Football Hall of Fame at the age of 34. He chose George Halas as his presenter.

He is a Pro Football Hall of Famer that never won a Super Bowl.

RIZE CASHMERE WITH CURRY AND FRUIT

1   pork tenderloin
1   package curry
    (Colman's, see page 150 for
    ordering information, – English,
    Madras – Indian, and Golden –
    Japanese)

White raisins, cranberries, or any dried
    fruit.

Milk, optional

Mango chutney, marmalade, cranberry/
    walnut chutney, or any coarse jam

Orzo, linguini, angel hair, penne, or bow
    tie pasta

Green seedless grapes, peaches,
    strawberries, sweet apple slices,
    pistachio, or cashew nuts,
    shredded coconut, or anything you
    like

This is a Swiss dish (rize means rice) from the Alps that mixes fruit, curry and pork. This recipe gives directions for pasta but certainly substitute white or brown rice if that is your choice. We ate this often when I was in Europe and it is my curry favorite.

Brown tenderloin in any pan deep enough to boil pasta in and transfer it to the oven for further cooking at 300 degrees for 20 minutes. If grilling on the grill, just cook it through. Either way, cut it open and if it's pink but not bloody, remove from heat, place on a cutting board and cover with foil; set aside. The pork will continue to cook on its own.

To make sauce: Prepare curry of your choice according to package directions adding white raisins or cranberries or any other dried fruit. If you cut the recommended water amount, after boiling you can add skim, regular milk or cream to make up the difference and gently heat so you don't burn the milk, for a creamier sauce, stirring well. Select the curry level of spice that suits you. The Golden Curry has different levels; the others a mild-medium with one choice. Don't be too afraid of the heat as the fruit and sweet chutney will off-set the heat somewhat.

Add mango chutney, marmalade, cranberry/walnut chutney (Honey Baked Ham), or any coarse jam. The Swiss use orzo but linguini, angel hair, penne, bow tie pastas are all fine. Colored pasta are always fun too. Cook the pasta of choice, being careful not to overcook as they all cook at a different pace.

Cut pork in cubes and toss all the above together. At the last, mix in halved grapes, anything in season, pistachio or cashew nuts, and shredded coconut. Garnish with any fruit with color. Serve.

BBQ PORK TENDERLOIN WITH GINGER MARINADE

1   lean pork tenderloin

*Chinablue scallion ginger glaze,
    Teriyaki marinade, or
    Wasabi ginger marinade

Pineapple chunks

*For ordering email
orders@thevirginiamarketplace.com

Place tenderloin in a mixing bowl and cover with marinade on both sides. Let pork soak as long as you like, even overnight if you like. Try to hold back some marinade for glazing as you cannot use what raw pork was soaking in as a final glaze. Grill, turning the pork, and when you think it might be done, cut into it on the grill. You want pink, not bloody. Remove from the grill to a clean cutting board. Cover with foil and set aside; it will continue to cook. Then slice pork in medallions and drizzle reserved marinade on each serving.

This pork is excellent with Teriyaki marinade mixed with pineapple juice. Garnish with pineapple chunks.

~Shay Griese

Don Shula

Don was coach of the Miami Dolphins; he led them to two Super Bowl victories. He was named 1993 Sportsman of the Year by Sports Illustrated and held the NFL record for most career wins.

SHULA'S STEAK SOUP

15 gallons

40	pounds Certified Angus Beef stew meat, cut into 1x1-inch cubes, trimmed and cleaned
1	cup fresh minced garlic
4	pounds carrots, medium diced
4	pounds onions, medium diced
4	pounds celery, medium diced
3	cups paprika
1	#10 can tomato paste
4	pounds all-purpose flour
10	gallons beef stock
3	#10 cans tomato purée
3	cups caraway seed, toasted
1	cup dry oregano
	Salt and pepper, to taste

Sear beef on all sides, add garlic and sauté.

Add carrots, onions, and celery; cook until lightly browned.

Add paprika and cook 5 minutes.

Add tomato paste and flour. Simmer for 10 minutes.

Add beef stock and bring to a boil. Reduce heat and simmer for 10-15 minutes.

Add tomato purée, toasted caraway seeds, and oregano. Simmer for 45 minutes.

Adjust seasoning with salt and pepper.

Cool in ice bath.

Store in appropriate containers until ready to reheat for service.

Don Shula was born on January 1, 1930, in Grand River, Ohio and graduated from John Carroll University. He earned a Master of Arts degree in Physical Education from Case Western Reserve University in 1954. Though he never started during his early playing career, Don signed with the Cleveland Browns as a defensive back. He played with the Browns from 1951-1952, the Baltimore Colts 1953-1956, and the Washington Redskins in 1957. Altogether, Don amassed 21 interceptions and 4 fumbles as a player.

As a coach Don made his indelible mark on the game. He served as a Defensive Coordinator for the Detroit Lions from 1960-1962, then took over as head coach for the Baltimore Colts from 1963-1969. After his stint with the Colts, Don took the position as Head Coach of the Miami Dolphins from 1970-1995. During his time with the Dolphins, Shula cemented himself as one of the greatest coaches ever to coach in the NFL. With Bob Griese at the helm, the Dolphins took home 2 Super Bowl trophies, VII and VIII. Shula was a 5 time AFC Championship winner, a 14 time divisional winner, and 4 time Coach of the Year winner. He has the most regular season wins by a head coach with 328, the most Super Bowl appearances as a head coach with 6, All-Time leader in victories with 347, most games coached with 526 and most consecutive seasons coached with 33.

I don't know any other way to lead but by example.
~Shula Quote

DON
SHULA

CROCKPOT BEEF STROGANOFF

1   prepackaged beef tips in gravy
      (Hormel® with no preservatives)

Red wine

Sour cream

Cooked broad egg noodles

Mushrooms

Pepper

Onion, sautéed (optional)

If you are in a hurry you can follow the microwave directions to heat, then add some red wine and finish with a dollop of sour cream served over cooked and buttered noodles.

If you have time, use the crockpot on low, add beef tips in gravy, mushrooms, red wine, pepper, and sautéed onion if using. Finish the same way with sour cream and noodles served in a shallow bowl.

CROCKPOT BEEF STEW

Use the same beef tips or a beef roast. If time permits you can place the tips in the crockpot frozen with a little bouillon. Add baby carrots, corn sheared off the cob, loosely chopped red peppers, pearl onions, fresh ground pepper, couple dashes of powdered garlic, and a couple ounces red wine. If the tips are frozen, cook for 30 minutes or until thawed, then add the veggies. Serve with mashed potatoes.

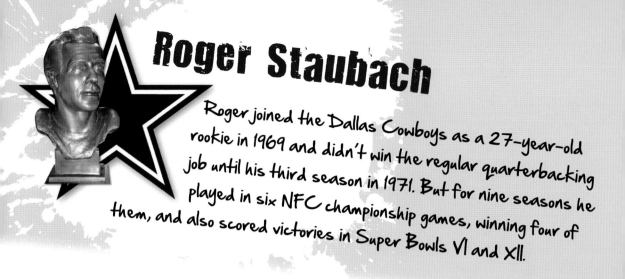

Roger Staubach

Roger joined the Dallas Cowboys as a 27-year-old rookie in 1969 and didn't win the regular quarterbacking job until his third season in 1971. But for nine seasons he played in six NFC championship games, winning four of them, and also scored victories in Super Bowls VI and XII.

CHICKEN POT PIE

Makes 2 (8-inch) pies or 4 (6-inch) pies

1   cup chopped onion
1   cup chopped celery
1   cup chopped carrots
⅓   cup butter
½   cup flour (self-rising or all-purpose)
2   cups chicken broth
1⅔ cups milk
4   cups cooked chicken
1½ cups frozen peas
1   teaspoon salt
¼   teaspoon pepper
1   tablespoon sugar
4   pie crusts

Sauté onions, celery, and carrots in butter until tender. Add flour; stir and cook 1 minute. Add chicken broth and milk. Cook and stir until thickened and bubbly. Stir in chicken, peas, salt, pepper, and sugar.

Line pie pans with crust; divide filling between the two. Cover with pie crust, seal edges of pie crust together, and slit tops for steam. Cover the edges with foil until the last 10 minutes. Freeze unbaked for up to 3 months. Cook frozen on cookie sheet at 400 degrees for 1½ hours.

CHICKEN – CHEESE AND WINE

1   can cream of chicken soup
¼   cup white wine
6-8   boneless chicken breasts
1   pound sliced Swiss cheese
1½-2 cups Pepperidge Farm® dressing
½   stick butter or margarine, melted

In a bowl, mix soup and wine until well blended. Place a small amount into a 9x13-inch Pyrex pan. Place chicken in pan; add Swiss cheese slices on top of chicken. Pour remaining soup mixture over chicken and cheese. Sprinkle herb dressing on top and drizzle with melted butter. Bake at 350 degrees for 1 hour. Serve with cooked rice.

COWBOYS

DID YOU KNOW?

Roger led the NFL in passing four times. He was also an All-NFC choice five times and selected to play in six Pro Bowls.

Staubach first starred as a quarterback at the U.S. Naval Academy, where he was a Heisman Trophy winner as a junior in 1963. Following graduation, he spent a mandatory four years on active duty, including service in Vietnam, before he was able to turn his attention to pro football.

Roger Staubach

Staubach wound up his career after the 1979 season with an 8,304 passing rating, the best mark by an NFL passer up to that time. His career chart shows 1,685 completions in 2,958 passing attempts, which were good for 22,700 yards and 153 touchdowns.

GLAZED STRAWBERRY PIE

1   (3-ounce) package cream cheese, softened
1   (9-inch) pie shell, baked
1   quart drained hulled strawberries
1½ cups strawberry juice
1   cup sugar
3   tablespoons cornstarch
½   pint heavy cream, whipped

Spread cream cheese over bottom of baked pie shell. Cover with half of the strawberries. Mash remaining berries and strain until juice is extracted. Add water if necessary to make 1½ cups of juice. Pour juice in a small saucepan and bring to a boil; stir in sugar and cornstarch. Cook over low heat, stirring constantly until mixture comes to a boil. Boil for 1 minute. Pour over berries in pie shell. Cool 2 hours. Before serving, decorate with whipped cream.

Note: If desired, juice may be cooked slowly for 10 minutes, stirring occasionally rather than boiled. Cool before pouring over berries.

DID YOU KNOW?

Roger Staubach was born on February 5, 1942, in Cincinnati, Ohio. He graduated from NAVY and won the 1963 Heisman Trophy. Because of his Naval commitments, he was drafted in 1964 but did not start playing until 1969 for the Cowboy's making him a 27 year old Rookie. From 1969-1979, Staubach quarterbacked the Cowboys to two Super Bowl victories in VI and XII. He was MVP in Super Bowl VI, a 6 time Pro Bowler, and a 1985 inductee into the Pro Football Hall of Fame. Staubach is regarded to most as the greatest Cowboy to have ever played. Coaches and team-mates alike gave Staubach a couple of different nicknames, "Captain America" and "Captain Comeback" because of his uncanny ability to lead his team to victories when others believed them to be down and out.

During Staubach's finest years with the Cowboys, Roger had the reputation for making the big play. He was the MVP of Super Bowl VI. He led Dallas Cowboys to their first Super Bowl victory. His is one of four who has won the Heisman Trophy and Super Bowl MVP. Super Bowl Champion (VI, XII) Hall of Fame 1985. His Dallas Cowboys career was from 1969-1979.

SHAY GRIESE'S
SIGNATURE SEA BASS WITH CHUTNEY

4   Sea Bass fillets, spine and bones removed (any good fresh white fish can be used)

2   teaspoons cinnamon

2   teaspoons cumin

2   teaspoon ginger

4   tablespoons Italian breadcrumbs

Olive oil, for coating and cooking

Get the thickest part of the fish and cut across the spine 2-3-inches apart. Cut out the spine and feel for bones all around the spine. They are easy to feel if they are there. You can remove them with needle-nose pliers. This will leave you with palm-sized chunks of thick fillets. Rinse the fillets. In a large mixing bowl add cinnamon, cumin, ginger, and breadcrumbs. Pat fish fillets dry, then dredge in olive oil on all sides; coat in the dry mixture. Set aside on a plate and refrigerate.

Clearly the favorite recipe that comes from my kitchen. It's super easy and well worth the try. Buy the freshest sea bass you can find since it is Chilean it is sometimes hard to get but any fish monger should be able to help you.

CHUTNEY

2   cups fresh squeezed orange juice

1   cup chopped pecans

3   tablespoons honey

White raisins

In a saucepan, add orange juice, pecans, and honey; simmer covered over medium heat until pecans are softened. Be careful not to let it boil over! When you are ready to start the sea bass, add white raisins; regular ones will darken the chutney. The raisins soak up the remaining liquid, so simmer until this happens, adding more until it thickens. Remove from heat and leave covered.

In a large Teflon skillet, coated in olive oil over medium-low heat, warm oil and skillet. Add chunks of sea bass. Depending on the thickness of the fish, cook one side for 10-15 minutes then flip. Try not to mess with the fish during this process as you can break it apart. If it holds together well when the other side is browned you can do the sides but this doesn't always work and it is not necessary. If the fish is very thick go another 10 minutes and reduce the heat. You can also cover it if you are unsure of the interior doneness, but it's better crispy so reduce the heat and be patient. You can keep the sea bass warm in the oven and use the same pan to sauté asparagus, adding butter until they are fork tender. If you don't prepare the asparagus, serve right away.

Serve with mashed potatoes (Country Crock® are good) oven heated in a foil-lined pan covered with pats of butter on top and pepper; lightly covered with foil; not labor intensive at all. Serve with chutney on the side.

Make enough chutney for the mornings; it is fantastic with cottage cheese and keeps well refrigerated.

~Shay Griese

SALMON WITH HOT SAUCE

Salmon fillets, skinless

Chef Prudhomme Blackened Redfish
    seasoning

Hot sauce

Slice across the spine of the filets in 2-inch widths to the tail. In a small bowl, make a paste of seasoning and hot sauce. If using the oven, preheat oven to 350 degrees. Using your fingers, coat 1 side only of each fillet with the paste. Wrap each individually and well. Place each on preheated grill for 7 minutes each side or 15 minutes in the preheated oven. Serve.

Great with rice and a salad. Don't worry about it being too hot, the oil in the salmon will neutralize the sauce.

~Shay Griese

CRAB CAKES

3-4 green onions, finely chopped

½ red bell pepper

4-5 tablespoons butter

¼ cup breadcrumbs

Seasonings of you choice, Emerils or
  Chef Prudhomme's

Juice of 1 lime

⅓ cup mayonnaise

1   pound lump crabmeat

Dijon mustard

Hot sauce or cocktail sauce

Sauté finely chopped green onions, both the white and green parts, and red pepper in butter until tender. Transfer to a large mixing bowl. Add breadcrumbs seasoned with your favorite seasoning. Add lime juice and mayonnaise. Mix well. Mix in the crab very delicately with your fingers, trying not to break them up. Once combined, make patties the size of hamburgers and about 1-inch thick. You need to do your best to keep the large crab chunks together as you are not using much filler. Refrigerate 2 to 3 hours to keep patties from falling apart.

In a skillet, heat oil on medium heat. Cook patties on both sides until brown. Serve with your favorite sauce.

SHRIMP CAKES

Same prep as above but use small thawed cooked shrimp with tails off.

Larry Csonka

Csonka, who was born in Stow, Ohio, on December 25, 1946, startled the pro football world by playing out his option with Miami in 1974 and then joining the Memphis' Southmen of the World Football League. Larry Csonka, a classic 6-3, 235-pound line-smashing fullback, provided the major rushing thrust in the Miami Dolphins' vaunted ball-control offense when the team was dominating the National Football League in the early 1970s.

CSONKA'S ALASKAN CHILI

1   large onion, chopped

1   green bell pepper, chopped

2-3 cloves garlic, chopped

Oil

2   pounds ground moose
     (or other ground game or beef)

1   pound ground moose chorizo
     (or ground sausage of your choice)

Baby bella mushrooms, sliced

Black olives, sliced

3   jars salsa

1   jar spaghetti sauce

1   can dark red kidney beans or pinto
     beans, rinsed will

1   can black beans or beans of your
     choice, rinsed well

1-2 fresh whole tomatoes, chopped

Red pepper flakes, to taste

Water, as needed

Sauté onion, bell pepper, and garlic in oil until tender. Add meat and brown; add mushrooms, black olives, salsa, spaghetti sauces, beans, tomatoes and red pepper flakes. Bring to a boil, reduce heat, cover and simmer for 30 minutes to 1 hour. Add water if needed.

Garnish with a dollop of sour cram, shredded Cheddar cheese and chopped cilantro if desired.

Audrey and I make this recipe from scratch so it's a little different each time. I like my chili thick and meaty so you might want extra salsa, sauce or water on hand to thin it out if you like more juice. You can also add ketchup for more tomato flavor.

112

DID YOU KNOW?

All-America at Syracuse and the Dolphins' No.1 draft pick in 1968, Larry contributed almost picture-perfect performances to Miami's three Super Bowl seasons in 1971, 1972, and 1973. Csonka surpassed 1,000 yards in rushing all three seasons with his best production - 1,117 yards - coming during Miami's perfect season in 1972. Larry earned All-AFC honors four times and was named All-Pro in 1971, 1972, and 1973.

Perhaps his finest single-game effort came in Super Bowl VIII, when he was selected as the game's Most Valuable Player. Csonka carried 33 times for a then–Super Bowl record 145 yards and two touchdowns. Larry wound up his 11-year career with 8,081 yards rushing and added 820 yards on 106 pass receptions.

Extremely sure-handed, he fumbled only 21 times in 11 seasons. His 408 points came on 68 touchdowns. Csonka's final fling proved to be a success. His 873 yards rushing was his best since 1973 and his 13 total touchdowns and 12 touchdowns rushing both were career highs.

LARRY CSONKA

FRUIT COBBLER

1   package World Famous® Mixes
    (see page 149 for ordering)

Strawberries, blueberries, peaches or
    fruit of your choice

World Famous Mixes, Inc. in Brandon,
MS. Makes the most amazingly easy
cobbler mix. Just follow the directions on
the package and add fresh strawberries,
blueberries, peaches or anything you
like that is in season. Out of season, use
frozen raspberries or blueberries from
the grocery store, but I usually freeze
my own.

SHAY'S FOOL-PROOF BREAD PUDDING

½-¾   loaf bread, of your choice

3-4   eggs

¼   cup maple syrup

Cinnamon, to taste

Any bread that you have that you need to use up
except rye and an equal portion of raisin cinnamon
bread amounting to ½-¾ of a loaf of bread,
depending on your needs.

Break bread into thumb-sized pieces and set
aside. Don't worry about it being stale or fresh, it
doesn't seem to matter. In a large mixing bowl, beat
eggs, maple syrup, and cinnamon to taste, then
add bread. Transfer the mixture to a non-stick loaf
pan coated with cooking spray and dusted with
flour or a buttered and floured loaf pan. Bake at
300 degrees for 40 minutes. The cooking time can
vary depending on the thickness of the loaf but
you will know when it's firm to the touch. Slice
and serve with butter, maple syrup, ice cream, or
whipped cream.

SAUTÉ SPINACH

2   tablespoons olive oil

Bagged baby spinach

Ground sea salt, to taste

Ground pepper, to taste

Tip: Do this dish in the same pan as was used for the main dish to save clean up and sauté the spinach at the very last to avoid overcooking, generally while you're tossing the salad.

Heat olive oil in a large saucepan over medium-low heat. Fill the pan with baby spinach. Stir with tongs until slightly wilted, then add ground sea salt and ground pepper to taste.

SPINACH SALAD

1   bag baby spinach, roughly chopped

1   red onion, finely chopped

Pecans or almonds, chopped

Apples, thinly sliced

Strawberries

Hearts of palm

1   hard-boiled egg, chopped

Hartville Kitchen Raspberry Sweet & Sour, or dressing of your choice (see page 149 for ordering information.)

Place spinach in a cold salad bowl. On top, arrange a red onion, pecans or almonds, apples, strawberries, hearts of palm, and egg. Mix with Hartville Kitchen Raspberry Sweet & Sour or any dressing of your choice. Toss and serve right away as the vinegar will wilt the spinach.

Steve Young

Steve is a former American college and professional football player who was a quarterback in the NFL for fourteen seasons during the 1980s and 1990s. He is a member of the College Football Hall of Fame and the Pro Football Hall of Fame.

MUSTARD GLAZED CARROTS

2   pounds carrots, scraped or peeled, cut in julienne strips
1   teaspoon salt
6   tablespoons butter
6   tablespoons prepared mustard
½   cup brown sugar

Cook carrots in boiling water with salt. While carrots are cooking, mix butter, mustard, and brown sugar in a pan and cook until syrupy.

Drain carrots, pour syrup over, and simmer 5 minutes.

MOM'S CHOCOLATE CHIP COOKIES

4   cups all-purpose flour
2   teaspoons baking soda
1   cup oatmeal
2   teaspoons salt
1½ cups granulated sugar
1½ cups packed brown sugar
2   cups butter
2   teaspoons vanilla
4   large eggs
1   (12-ounce) package chocolate chips
    Nuts

In a bowl, combine flour, baking soda, oatmeal, and salt. In a large mixing bowl, combine sugars, butter, and vanilla; beat until creamy. Add eggs one at a time. Gradually add flour mixture. Stir in chips and nuts.

Bake at 375 degrees for 9-11 minutes. Cool on wire rack if they last long enough.

DID YOU KNOW?

Quarterback Steve Young entered the National Football League through the 1984 supplemental draft. After spending two seasons in the ill-fated United States Football League, the consensus All-American from Brigham Young was selected by the Tampa Bay Buccaneers in first round of the special draft.

In 1987, Young was traded to the San Francisco 49ers where he served as the backup to Hall of Famer Joe Montana. After seeing limited action in his first four seasons with the 49ers, Young stepped into the starting role in 1991, after Montana suffered an injury. Young wasted little time in taking command of the 49ers offense. Despite a knee injury that forced him out of five games that season, Young passed for 2,517 yards and 17 touchdowns to post a league high 101.8 passer rating – the first of four straight passing titles. Young added two more passing titles in 1996 and 1997 to tie him with the legendary Sammy Baugh as the only quarterbacks in history to win six NFL passing crowns.

His finest season came in 1994 when he posted a then-record 112.8 passer rating by completing 324 of 461 passes for 3,969 yards and 35 touchdowns. Young also added seven rushing touchdowns as he guided the 49ers to a NFC West title with a 13-3 record. The team then coasted through the postseason. In the NFC championship game that year, Young threw two touchdowns and rushed for one as the 49ers downed the Dallas Cowboys 38-28. He topped off the year with an incredible performance in San Francisco's 49-26 win over the San Diego Chargers in Super Bowl XXIX. Young passed for 325 yards and threw a Super Bowl record six touchdowns. He also was the game's leading rusher with 49 yards on five carries. For his efforts, he was named the Super Bowl Most Valuable Player.

During his NFL career, the left-hander threw for 3,000 or more yards six times and had 20 or more touchdown passes in a season five times, and posted a passer rating of 100 or higher six times. Aside from his passing ability, Young was a constant threat as a runner. He ran for 4,239 yards and scored 43 rushing touchdowns.

Young, one of the most accurate passers in league history, was named All-Pro in 1992, 1993, 1994, and 1998, and earned All-NFC honors three times. The two-time league MVP also was selected to the Pro Bowl seven times.

STEVE YOUNG

SIMPLE SHEPHERD'S PIE

2   pounds lean ground beef
1   white onion, chopped
2   cups beef bouillon
Frozen mixed vegetables
1   package gravy mix
1   pie crust, premade
Mashed potatoes

In a sauté pan, add ground beef and onion, breaking the beef up as you sauté until meat is cooked through and onions are soft. Add bouillon to infuse more flavor and boil in the liquid. The longer you cook the meat, the better the flavor.

Add frozen mixed vegetables and boil off the liquid. The longer you cook it, the better it will taste. Prepare gravy mix according to package directions that you like. (I like Colman's® Shepherd's Pie Sauce Mix but use a little less liquid than the directions call for.) Add to beef mixture, continue cooking until liquid is evaporated.

In a pre-made pie crust add the beef mixture and coat with mashed potatoes (pre-made grocery store potatoes are great and easy and provide different flavors). Bake at 325 degrees for 1 hour but cover lightly with a sheet of foil so the crust doesn't brown too quickly. Once warmed through, which you can test with a meat thermometer, let rest in the open oven with no heat to set up for about 15 minutes. Serve with a nice, simple green salad. Since this dish is already cooked, it is a good meal to pre-make, refrigerate or freeze and microwaves well when you are in a hurry.

Typically, this dish is not made with beef. The end result though is easy and hearty.

ROASTED BABY POTATOES

Multi-colored potatoes

Worcestershire sauce

½   stick butter

Olive oil

Salt

Pepper

Garlic powder (optional)

Hot sauce, to taste (optional)

Dried rosemary

Halve or quarter potatoes depending on the size, but the goal is bite size. In a foil lasagna size pan with high sides, mix potatoes, splashes of Worcestershire sauce, butter, drizzle of olive oil, salt, pepper, and if you desire, garlic powder and hot sauce to taste. Mix and bake covered with foil at 275 degrees for 5 minutes. Remove from oven and stir in dried rosemary and mix in the butter. Remove the cover and bake until potatoes are fork tender and serve.

You can do the same thing with asparagus but leave off the sauces.

FENNER'S GREAT SOUP

1-2 pounds lean ground beef

1 onion

Mushrooms, chopped

Olive oil

1 can original Rotel®, undrained

¼ cup white wine

1 cup chopped fresh or frozen assorted vegetables

Pepper

1 beef bouillon cube

Orzo pasta

In a soup pot sauté ground beef, onion, and mushrooms. Add in a splash of olive oil over low heat. Add Rotel, white wine, vegetables, pepper, and bouillon cube. When the veggies are soft, add a handful of orzo pasta. Cook until the orzo is soft. For a thicker soup, use more pasta.

Tip: If you have time this soup does well for a couple of hours in a crockpot and you can use barley instead but you need 2 hours to soften the barley.

MEATBALLS

Makes 8 (4 ounce) meatballs

1½ pounds ground beef

½ pound ground pork

1 ounce breadcrumbs

2 eggs

½ ounce fresh minced garlic

1 ounce grated Parmesan cheese

Salt and pepper, to taste

Mix all ingredients and adjust seasoning.

Form into desired size.

In a hot sauté pan sear the meatballs until golden brown and delicious. Finish in the oven until cooked through.

Serve with your favorite marinara sauce and Parmesan cheese.

Recommended wine pair with IL Poggione Rosso di Montalcino

Submitted by
Chef Dominics of
Grafitto's in Wellington,
Florida

TOMATOES FOR BRUSCHETTA

2 pints cherry tomatoes

3 ounces extra-virgin olive oil

3 ounces barley malt

10 sprigs fresh thyme

JAM

5 pounds tomatoes

2 ounces soy sauce

5 ounces brown sugar

Wash tomatoes and cut them in half. Mix olive oil and barley together and toss with tomatoes. Cover with thyme sprigs and roast at 350 degrees for 20-30 minutes.

For the jam: make an x with a small knife on the bottom of the tomatoes; blanch tomatoes in a pot of boiling water until the skin starts to peel off. Shock in a bowl of ice water then peel, seed and small dice tomatoes in a saucepan. Add soy sauce and sugar; cook on low heat until almost all the liquid has evaporated.

Submitted by Chef Dominics of Grafitto's in Wellington, Florida

CHICKEN SALTIMBOCCA

4 Tyson® chicken breast

Salt and pepper, to taste

5 cups milk

1 cup polenta

4 ounces butter

8 sage leafs

4 ounces fontina cheese

Salt and pepper, to taste

2 ounces prosciutto

Season chicken with salt and pepper. In a skillet with oven proof handle, pan sear chicken and finish in the oven at 400 degrees for 12-15 minutes.

In a saucepan, bring milk to a simmer and add polenta. When polenta is almost finished, turn the heat off and add butter, sage, and fontina cheese and mix well. Season with salt and pepper.

To assemble the dish: place polenta in the middle of the plate, place chicken on top and garnish with prosciutto.

Recommended wine pair with La Vis pinot noir

Submitted by Chef Dominics of Grafitto's in Wellington, Florida

POTATO SALAD

1   pound small creamers potatoes
½   cup chopped red onion
¼   cup chopped cilantro or parsley

DRESSING

½   cup lemon juice
2   tablespoons extra virgin olive oil
1   teaspoon finely chopped garlic
Pinch sea salt
Pinch freshly ground black pepper

In a pot, add enough water to cover potatoes and bring to a boil and cook until fork tender. Drain. Add onion, cilantro or parsley; set aside.

In a small bowl combine all dressing ingredients. Mix well and pour over salad. Toss well and chill before serving.

Submitted by RoKaya McGarry from Morocco

EGGPLANT SALAD

2-3 eggplants
4-6 tomatoes, peeled and small diced
1   onion, chopped
½   cup extra virgin olive oil
Pinch sea salt
Pinch paprika
Pinch cumin
Pinch black pepper
1   teaspoon chopped garlic
¼   cube Knorr® chicken bouillon
1   tablespoon hot sauce, optional

Cut eggplant in half and place in a pot of boiling water, cook until tender but not soft. Drain and remove skin and mince.

In a frying pan, over medium heat, add tomatoes, onion, olive oil, salt, paprika, cumin, pepper, garlic, and bouillon. Cook until heated through. Stir in eggplant, reduce heat to low and add hot sauce if using.

Submitted by RoKaya McGarry from Morocco

TOMATO CUCUMBER SALAD

SALAD

5   medium-size tomatoes, cut in small
    pieces

2   roasted green or red peppers

1   English seedless cucumber, cut in
    small pieces

½   cup fresh cilantro
    (may substitute parsley)

¼   cup olives, any type
    (preferred Kalamata Greek olives)

DRESSING

2-3 tablespoons pure extra-virgin olive
    oil

3-4 cloves garlic

Fresh ground black pepper

¼   cup Kalamata olive juice

Pinch sea salt and pepper

In a large bowl, add tomatoes, roasted peppers, cucumber, cilantro, and olives; set aside. Using a food processor, add olive oil, garlic, pepper, olive juice, and salt and pepper to taste; process until well blended. Pour over vegetables; mix well and chill.

Both recipes submitted by RoKaya McGarry from Morocco

CARROT SALAD

4   cups shredded carrots

2   cups freshly squeezed orange juice

1   orange peeled, cut into wedges

1   tablespoon Orange Blossom water,
    optional

1   cup gold raisins

1   teaspoon cinnamon

Mix all ingredients and chill before serving.

TOMATO MOZZARELLA SALAD

Serves 4

2 pints cherry tomatoes

3 ounces extra-virgin olive oil

3 ounces honey

10 sprigs fresh thyme

4 ounces arugula

1 ounce shaved red onion

1 ounce shaved fennel

3 egg yolks

6 ounces balsamic vinegar

2 cups extra-virgin olive oil

Salt and black pepper, to taste

1 pound fresh mozzarella

Half tomatoes and toss with olive oil, honey, and thyme sprigs. Roast in the oven at 400 degrees for 25-30 minutes.

Mix arugula, red onion and fennel in a bowl.

To make the balsamic dressing: blend egg yolks and balsamic. Slowly add olive oil in a stream to make a creamy consistency. Season with salt and pepper.

To assemble the dish: mix greens with desired amount of dressing. Place on a plate and garnish with oven roasted tomatoes and fresh mozzarella.

Recommended wine pair with Asoria Prosecco

Submitted by Chef Dominics of Grafitto's in Wellington, Florida

FETTUCCINI ALFREDO WITH VEGETABLES

1   package fettuccini noodles
Asparagus tips
Roasted red peppers
Olives in olive oil
Fresh spinach, finely chopped
Cream
Parmesan cheese, divided
Capers for garnish

Prepare fettuccini noodles according to package directions. Sauté asparagus tips, roasted red peppers, and olives in olive oil. When asparagus are done, add fresh spinach. Drain noodles and place in a large serving bowl with butter. Add cream and Parmesan cheese; toss. Add vegetables and toss again. Garnish with caper and additional Parmesan cheese. Serve.

SWEET POTATOES WITH MAPLE SYRUP

1   onion, chopped
1   package Country Crock® prepared
     sweet potatoes
Butter, to taste
Maple syrup, to taste

Sauté onion and set aside. Heat prepared sweet potatoes. Mix in butter, sautéed onion, and maple syrup. Serve.

TENDERLOIN SANDWICH APPETIZERS

Whole beef tenderloin
Sea salt and peppercorn medley
Sister Schubert's® yeast rolls
Horseradish and Dijonnaise

Season tenderloin with sea salt and peppercorn; place on broiler pan in 500 degree oven for 30 minutes. Turn oven off, keeping oven closed and leave roast in for additional 30 minutes. While cooling, place Sister Schubert's yeast rolls in oven, per directions. Slice tenderloin and serve on rolls with horseradish and Dijonnaise.

Recipe submitted by
Carrie Dobbs

SPUNKY CAESER SALAD

HOMEMADE CROUTONS

Olive oil

Garlic powder

Pepper

White or sourdough bread, cut in chunks

Prepare frying pan with olive oil seasoned with garlic powder and pepper. Add bread chunks; mix until toasted. Set aside.

SALAD

Hearts of Romaine lettuce

Cut stalk, wash and wrap in paper towel to drain; refrigerate to chill.

SAUCE

Big squeeze Reese® Anchovy Paste, dash mayonnaise, olive oil, fresh lemon cut in half and juiced, liberally add fresh Parmesan cheese, minced garlic and red wine vinegar.

OLD FASHIONED HONEY WHEAT BREAD

2 loaves

1½ cups cream style cottage cheese or ricotta cheese

½ cup honey

¼ cup butter

5½-6 cups all-purpose or unbleached flour

1 cup whole wheat flour

2 tablespoons sugar

3 teaspoons salt

2 packages active dry yeast

1 egg

Heat first 4 ingredients in a medium saucepan until very warm (120-130 degrees). Lightly spoon flour into measuring cup; level off. Combine warm liquid, 2 cups of the flour and remaining ingredients in a large bowl; beat 2 minutes at medium speed. By hand stir in remaining flour to make a stiff dough.

Knead dough on well-floured surface, until smooth and elastic, about 2 minutes. Place in a greased bowl. Cover. Let rise in warm place until light and doubled in size, about 45 to 60 minutes.

Grease 2 (9x5-inch) pans or 2 (8x4-inch) pans. Punch down the dough. Divide and shape into 2 loaves. Tuck under the sides of each portion and place dough into the greased pans. Cover again and let rise in warm place until light and doubled in size.

Preheat oven to 350 degrees. Bake 40 to 50 minutes until deep golden brown and loaves sound hollow when lightly tapped. Immediately remove from pans. If desired, brush warm loaves with butter.

Submitted by
Kay K Borkowski

BROCCOLI SALAD

SALAD
Broccoli florets
Pine nuts or sesame seeds
Bacon or ham, cooked

DRESSING
Mayonnaise
Red wine vinegar
Balsamic vinegar
Honey or sugar
Cranberries or raisins

Chop broccoli, add pine nuts or sesame seeds, precooked bacon or ham; set aside.

To make dressing: In a bowl, add mayonnaise, vinegars, honey or sugar; mix well. Pour dressing over broccoli and let stand. Boil cranberries or raisins and add before serving.

BASIC BALSAMIC DRESSING

Balsamic vinegar
Olive oil
Dijon mustard
Honey
Mayonnaise
Salt and pepper, to taste

In a bowl, whisk together vinegar and olive oil. Add Dijon mustard, honey, mayonnaise and whisk. Add salt and pepper to taste.

Recommend using
McCormick Mayonnaise
infused with lime.

LASAGNA

Beef

Onions

Peppers

1   teaspoon minced garlic

Bertolli Tomato Basil

Lowes Generic tomato sauce, optional

Gourmet Garden Basil, squeeze

Barilla Lasagna, no boil

Mozzarella cheese, slices

Ricotta cheese

Sauté beef, onions, pepper, and garlic until beef is fully cooked but not browned. Add Bertolli tomato basil and continue to cook; if too dry add Lowes Generic Tomato sauce. Add a squeeze of Gourmet Garden Basil. Cook all day if you can to infuse the flavors into the meat.

When ready take an aluminum lasagna pan, start with thin layer of sauce. Layer with Barilla Lasagna, no boiling required pasta. Cover with mozzarella cheese slices, then coat with Ricotta cheese. Add another layer of noodles, sauce, noodles, and cheeses. Repeat the process until 1-inch from the top. Cover with sauce as the cheese will burn. Bake at 350 degrees for 1½ hours at most. Let rest before cutting, uncovered 15 minutes.

LAMB BURGERS

Fresh ground lamb

Breadcrumbs

Mayonnaise

Mint Jelly

Toasted onion buns

Mix ground lamb with breadcrumbs; form into patties. Grill or sauté on stove. Serve with mayonnaise mixed with mint jelly on a toasted onion bun.

CURRY SHRIMP AND ORZO PASTA

Orzo pasta

Peppers

Shallots or onion

Asparagus or green vegetable of choice

Olive oil

Shrimp

Cream or milk

Curry powder

Salt and pepper, to taste

In a pot, boil orzo pasta, drain and set aside. In the same pot sauté peppers, shallots or onion, asparagus or green vegetable of your choice in olive oil. Add shrimp that has been thawed but previously cooked found in your freezer section and remove tails. Throw all together; add cream or milk, curry powder, (recommend Original Sun Brand Madras Curry Powder), salt, and pepper to taste.

GREEN CABBAGE

1   head cabbage

Butter

Salt and pepper, to taste

Slice cabbage and sauté in water with butter, salt, and pepper. Reduce heat to low, cover and cook for 2 hours.

HOMEMADE CROUTONS

Use white bread or sourdough store bought sandwich type. Cut in 1-inch crouton size chunks; prepare toast in a fry-pan, just coating the bottom with olive oil seasoned with garlic powder and pepper and salt. Turn until toasted. Set aside or store in zip top plastic bags to use later.

CORN CASSEROLE

1 stick butter
2 eggs
2 cans cream of corn
1 can corn, drained
1 cup sour cream
1 box Jiffy corn muffin mix

Melt butter and add eggs, cream of corn, corn, sour cream and muffin mix. Mix together, pour into greased pan and bake for 30 to 40 minutes at 350 degrees. Insert a toothpick until it comes out clean.

Recipe submitted by Maryann Griese

HOT PEPPER JELLY

½ cup finely chopped jalapeño
1½ cups sweet red and green peppers
6 cups sugar
1½ cups white vinegar
1 bottle or 2 envelopes Certo

In a saucepan, add jalapeños, and peppers; mix with sugar and vinegar. Bring to a boil and cook 3 minutes. Add Certo and continue to boil 1 minute more. Remove from heat and let rest 5 minutes. Skim and pour into small jars and seal.

HOTTER JELLY

1½ cups white vinegar
1 cup jalapeño
1 cup sweet peppers
6 cups sugar
1 bottle or 2 envelops certo

Directions are the same as above.

Recipe submitted by Ken Coleman

ZITI

2 pounds ground chuck

3 jars of your favorite spaghetti sauce

2 boxes penne noodles

2 eggs

2 pounds ricotta

2 bags Sargento 6 cheese Italian shredded cheese

2 bags shredded mozzarella

2 tablespoons parsley

2 tablespoons Italian seasoning

In a skillet, brown the ground chuck and make sure it is good and crumbly. In a slow cooker (on low) empty your jars of sauce. When ground chuck is ready, drain off grease, blot with a paper towel, and add to sauce in slow cooker. Boil noodles until slightly undercooked (a bit less than al dente). While noodles are boiling, preheat the oven to 375 degrees. Combine 2 eggs with ricotta, shredded cheese, 1 bag of mozzarella, parsley and Italian seasoning. Mix well with a spoon or hands. When noodles are ready, drain and rinse under cold water. In large lasagna pan, place sauce—enough to cover the bottom, so noodles do not stick. Then layer noodles cheese mixture/sauce and repeat until pan is full. Cover with foil loosely, place in the oven, and cook for 1 hour. It is ready when the noodles on top are ever so slightly crisp. Remove and garnish on top with mozzarella to your liking. Put the remaining sauce in the slow cooker, which is great for those who enjoy extra sauce or for dipping with a nice crusty Italian bread.

Recipe submitted by
Carrie Dobbs

134

CABBAGE ROLLS

1   large cabbage
1   cup rice, cooked
1   pounds ground beef
1   pound ground pork
1   onion, chopped and browned
Salt and pepper to taste
2-3 tablespoons ketchup
2-3 eggs
1   large can Heinz® tomato juice

Steam cabbage and separate leaves; set aside. Mix other ingredients by hand in a large bowl. Wrap handful of meat mixture with leaves. Place in large roasting pan. Pour juice over when all are finished. Place in oven at 350 degrees for 1 hour.

*Recipe submitted by
Suzanne Bax*

BLUEBERRY GÂTEAU

½   cup butter
1   cup plus 1 tablespoon sugar
2   eggs
1   cup plus 1 teaspoon flour
1   teaspoon baking powder
⅛   teaspoon salt
2   cups fresh blueberries
½   teaspoon lemon juice
1   tablespoon icing sugar

Cream butter and sugar until fluffy. Add eggs one at a time. Add flour, baking powder, and salt. Spray flan pan with nonstick cooking spray; spread dough evenly through out. Mix blueberries, 1 teaspoon flour and 1 tablespoon sugar together then add lemon juice; pour over batter. Place in oven at 350 degrees for 1 hour. When cooled, sift icing sugar over the flan. Delisssss.

H. Lee Moffitt

H. Lee Moffitt, an attorney and former state legislator, served as Speaker of the Florida House of Representatives from 1982 to 1984. A Tampa native and cancer survivor, he conceived the idea for the creation of the Cancer Center and spearheaded a $70-million appropriation through the Legislature to build the facility.

EASY GAZPACHO

2   cucumbers, partially peeled and chopped

2   red peppers, chopped into small squares

4-5 ripe plum tomatoes, lightly chopped

1   red onion, chopped

4   cloves garlic, chopped

3-4 cups vegetable juice, prefer V8

¼   cup red or white wine vinegar

¼   cup Alessi olive oil

½   tablespoon sugar

½   tablespoon Alessi sea salt

Pepper, to taste

Dash or two of Tabasco, to taste

2-3 tablespoons chopped parsley

Place everything into a food processor and blend gently – let it stay a bit chunky. Pour in covered container and chill; the longer the better.

DID YOU KNOW?

Throughout Mr. Moffitt's tenure in the Florida legislature, he labored for nine years on his dream: to bring to Florida a world-class cancer center, an institution where working for a cure would be as important as offering patients the most advanced treatment. During Moffitt's term as speaker, the Legislature named the cancer center after him, to recognize and honor him for his commitment to the initiative.

Mr. Moffitt earned his B.A. from the University of South Florida and his law degree from Cumberland School of Law.

Today, Mr. Moffitt donates much of his time to efforts related to the cancer center for cancer research, and his passion is serving on the board of the H. Lee Moffitt Cancer Center & Research Institute.

BANANA ROLL-UPS

2 slices white/wheat or plain white sandwich bread, crust removed

2 tablespoons smooth peanut butter

1 banana, peeled

Remove crust from bread. Spread peanut butter over both slices of bread, making sure both peanut butter sides are facing up; over lap one slice about ½-inch. The peanut butter will glue them together. Next, lay a peeled banana across one edge and roll it up tightly. Slice about 1-inch across the roll and serve.

When I was a little girl my mum used to make these for us on the off occasion we got home for lunch. Since our school was so far from our home she always tried to make it special and the roll-ups have stuck with me.
~Shay Griese

ICEBERG WEDGE

1   head iceberg lettuce, washed and
    drained

Blue cheese dressing

Blue cheese or Gorgonzola

Fresh ground pepper

Cut lettuce into 6 equal wedges. Pour blue cheese dressing over wedges. Sprinkle with blue or Gorgonzola cheese and add lots of fresh ground pepper. McCormick's Black Peppercorn Grinder is easy and fresh.

PUCCI'S PEPPERS AND SAUSAGE

2-3 pounds turkey or chicken Italian
    style sausage

Peppers of your choice

Sweet onion

Yukon gold potatoes, halved

Olive oil

Salt and pepper, to taste

Par boil sausage and cool then remove casing. Cut into bite-size pieces, about 1-inch. Chop peppers, onion, and potatoes; drizzle with olive oil and toss. Add salt and pepper to taste; toss again. Transfer to a baking pan. Bake at 375 degrees for 45 minutes, turning every 15 minutes.

A great product is Everglades Food, Inc. All-Purpose Seasoning. For ordering information see page 149.

BACKSTREETS (WELLINGTON, FL) GRILLED WRAPS

Mayonnaise

Relish, your choice

Mustard

Tortilla flatbread, your choice

Sandwich meat, thinly sliced*

Swiss cheese or your choice

Tomatoes, thinly sliced

In a small bowl, combine mayonnaise, relish and mustard; set aside. Lay soft tortilla flat and spread with mayonnaise mixture. Layer with meat, cheese, and tomato. Roll it together tightly.

Lightly oil a large skillet or flat pan. Heat skillet or flat pan over low heat. Add wrap and grill, turning until it is brown and toasted on all sides.

My preference is seasoned Boars Head ham, but turkey, roast beef or any meat is fine.

The reason why these are far better than what you buy is that they are grilled. It is a little more trouble but truly worth it. I send Bob with these when he travels and they are not messy and not doughy.

~Shay

WATERCRESS SALAD

Watercress
Red cabbage
Red wine vinegar
Olive oil
Salt
Fresh ground pepper, to taste
Onions (optional)

In a bowl, chop fresh watercress into bite-size pieces. Shred red cabbage of equal amount. Mix red wine vinegar and a good olive oil (1-2) ratio. Season with salt and pepper to taste; add to watercress cabbage mixture. Toss gently. Pile high on a plate and top with crispy onion, if using.

There is a restaurant in Bellagio Hotel called Prime that used to make an amazing salad. Here is my best interpretation.

RED CABBAGE

Red cabbage, chopped
Sugar
Vinegar
Applesauce

In a pot of water, add cabbage, sugar, vinegar, and apple sauce to taste. Cook until cabbage is tender. This takes a while to cook so add more water if needed. The key is the applesauce for a nice twist and it's great with grilled pork tenderloin and a potato or a seasoned boxed rice.

SHRIMP AND CHEESY GRITS

1 package instant grits
Shredded Cheddar cheese
Red peppers, thinly sliced
Frozen cooked shrimp tails, thawed
White wine
Oil

Prepare instant grits according to package directions but add a couple of handfuls Cheddar cheese. The microwave instructions are fine for this. In a skillet, briefly sauté red peppers and shrimp in enough white wine and a little oil to heat the shrimp and soften the peppers. Serve over grits and garnish with something green.

You can also use thinly sliced chicken but cook it through.

MANDARIN ORANGE CHICKEN OR PORK

1   can Mandarin oranges, undrained
2   tablespoons orange marmalade
1   teaspoon cornstarch
Dash soy sauce
Chicken breast or pork tenderloin

Prepare the sauce: In a saucepan, add Mandarin oranges with liquid, orange marmalade, cornstarch, and soy sauce. Set it aside. In a skillet, add a little oil and sauté chicken over high heat until it is browned, then flip. You can do the same on your grill but be careful with chicken as it gets dry. A lean pork tenderloin will not dry as easily on the grill but can also be done easily in your sauté pan. Slice chicken crossways and arrange on plate; pour on the sauce.

MASHED POTATOES

Country Crock™ potatoes
Sour cream
Butter, unsalted
Fresh herbs (basil or rosemary)

Add sour cream or unsalted butter and fresh herbs like basil or rosemary; heat according to directions.

These are excellent made into patties and pan-fried until crispy. Serve with eggs and sausage on Sunday morning.

Country Crock™ makes the best everything potato that will insure that you won't ever go through the task of doing your own.

STOVE TOP STEAKS

White onions

Baby bella mushrooms

Olive oil

Wine

Grain mustard

1   jar bruschetta (optional)

Rib-eye or filets of your choice

Crumbled blue cheese

Finely chop onion and slice mushrooms. Add enough olive oil in a skillet to coat the bottom. Sauté onion and mushrooms in skillet; when mushrooms soak up the moisture, add wine that you intend to drink with the meal and a good grain mustard. Continue to cook and boil down until it thickens a bit. Add bruschetta, if using. When the mixture has thickened, put on a plate and set aside.

Using the same skillet, reduce heat to medium-high and sear the steaks on both sides until preferred doneness. Remove steak to plates. Reheat the mushroom mixture in the same skillet for just a minute, coat the meat and sprinkle with blue cheese. Serve.

If you don't feel like firing-up the bar-b-que this is an easy, quick and reliable alternative.

PEACH CHUTNEY

Sweet onion, finely chopped
Butter
Brown sugar
Fresh peaches, chopped

In a skillet, sauté onion in butter and add brown sugar to taste, continuing to stir. Add fruit and cook until thickened. This chutney is great over grilled meat or cottage cheese cold in the morning.

Seasonal peaches are the only ingredient I would use but frozen blueberries, raspberries and strawberries work well.

AVOCADO AND SHRIMP LUNCH

Avocado

Small cooked shrimp

Mayonnaise

Seafood spice

Fresh lemon or lime juice

Fresh black pepper

Split a ripe avocado in half and remove the pit. Mix shrimp, mayonnaise, spices, a squeeze of lemon or lime juice, and black pepper. Stuff avocado halves liberally and serve.

PULLED PORK BAR-B-QUE SANDWICH

1   package Jack Daniel's® seasoned
    and cooked pulled pork

1   ounce bourbon

1   package hamburger buns

Sweet onion, sliced

Heat pork in a skillet according to package directions. If it doesn't come with whiskey added, then add bourbon; 1 ounce per package. Toast hamburger buns lightly. Pile meat on one half of bun; add a slice of onion and serve with slaw.

This can also be done with shredded chicken or beef.

Store bought slaw is usually good but if you want to make your own buy a bag of slaw from the produce and mix in a bowl with mayonnaise, apple cider or red wine vinegar, sweet relish and add salt and pepper to taste.

Photo from Jack Daniel's® Meats.
See product information on page 150.

BACON LETTUCE TOMATO SALAD

Bacon
Iceberg lettuce
Cherry tomatoes, halved
Lite Caesar salad dressing

Using scissors, cut bacon into bite-size pieces and cook until crispy. Set aside on paper towel to drain.

In a salad bowl, chop lettuce into bite-size pieces; add tomatoes halves. Using a good lite Caesar salad dressing, mix everything together, then sprinkle with lots of bacon.

Only make this salad the day of serving; cover with a damp paper towel and refrigerate. Knife cut lettuce browns overnight. Don't add dressing or bacon until ready to serve. Also, try to use a salad bowl that can be chilled, like glass. It's best if lettuce and dressing is very cold.

LANE'S BEEF BURGUNDY

Serves 8

3	pounds beef tip round steak (first cut), sliced ½-inch thick
½	cup flour
4	tablespoons butter
3	onions, chopped
1	4½-ounce jar sliced mushrooms
1	whole garlic clove
1	bay leaf
1	teaspoon salt

Pepper, to taste

3	tablespoons finely snipped parsley
2	cups burgundy wine
½	cup water, more if needed

Cut steak into bite-size cubes. Place in a zip-top bag with flour and shake to coat cubes. Melt butter in a large skillet. Add a few steak pieces at a time and brown on both sides (don't brown all the meat at once; do one skillet full at a time). Using the same skillet, add onion, mushrooms, garlic, bay leaf, salt, pepper, parsley, wine and water. Heat mixture to boiling; reduce heat and simmer covered about 1 hour or until meat is tender. Remove bay leaf and garlic clove.

Serve over hot, fluffy rice or hot, cooked noodles.

OUR FAVORITE PRODUCTS

2200 W. Don Tyson Pkwy
Springdale, AR 72762
479.290.4000 • www.tysonfoods.com

Tyson is a registered
trademark of Tyson Foods, Inc.

1015 Edison St. NW #1
Hartville, OH 44632
330.877.9353 • www.hartvillekitchen.com

2530 W. Broadway St.
Forrest City, AR 72335
870.630.1637 • www.boarshead.com

World Famous Fruit Cobbler Mix
1700 W. Government St., Ste B
Brandon, MS 39042-2420
601.825.7163 • www.jrschoicemixes.com

Everglades Foods, Inc.
441 Webster Turn Drive
Sebring, FL 33870
Tel: 800-689-2221
Fax: 863-655-4058
www.shop.evergladesseasoning.com

Swiss Chalet Dipping Sauce
www.swisschalet.com

Coleman
24 Elgin Lane, Palm Beach,
Gardens, FL 33418
561.379.5675

1-800-523-4635, 8 a.m. - 4 p.m. CT
Monday - Friday, excluding holidays.
Summer hours may vary.

www.hormelfoods.com

Hormel Foods Corporation
Consumer Response
1 Hormel Place
Austin, MN 55912

Jack Daniel's
Ready to Eat Meats
1-866-757-JACK (5225)
info@jackdanielsmeats.com

Title

Ingredients

Directions

Title

Ingredients

Directions

Title

Ingredients

Directions

Title

Ingredients

Directions

Title

Ingredients

Directions

Title

Ingredients

Directions

Title

Ingredients

Directions

Title

Ingredients

Directions

Title

Ingredients

Directions

Title

Ingredients

Directions

LIST OF CELEBRITIES

CELEBRITIES

APPETIZERS

ASPARAGUS

BEANS AND PEAS

BEEF

BREAKFAST

CABBAGE

CARROTS